Oh, the doors you will open!

HARCOURT SCHOOL PUBLISHERS

STORYtown

Rolling Along

Senior Authors

Isabel L. Beck • Roger C. Farr • Dorothy S. Strickland

Authors

Alma Flor Ada • Roxanne F. Hudson • Margaret G. McKeown
Robin C. Scarcella • Julie A. Washington

Consultants

F. Isabel Campoy • Tyrone C. Howard • David A. Monti

SCHOOL PUBLISHERS

www.harcourtschool.com

Rolling Along

Harcourt
SCHOOL PUBLISHERS

www.harcourtschool.com

Theme **1**

Count on Me

Contents

★ **Language Arts** **Lesson 1**

Paired Selections

Social Studies

Theme Writing **Reading-Writing Connection** 52
Student Writing Model: Personal Narrative

Social Studies **Lesson 2**

Paired Selections

Science

Theme 2
Doing Our Best

Contents

Theme 3
Changing Times

Contents

Visual Arts

Lesson 11

Paired Selections

Language Arts

Theme Writing — **Reading-Writing Connection**

Student Writing Model: Friendly Letter

Social Studies

Lesson 12

Paired Selections

Social Studies

Comprehension Strategies

Before You Read

Think about what you already know.
Look over the words and pictures before you read.

Set a purpose.
Decide why you are reading.

I want to enjoy reading a story.

While You Read

Use story structure.
Think about a story's characters, setting, and plot.

Use graphic organizers.
Use a story map, web, or chart to help you read.

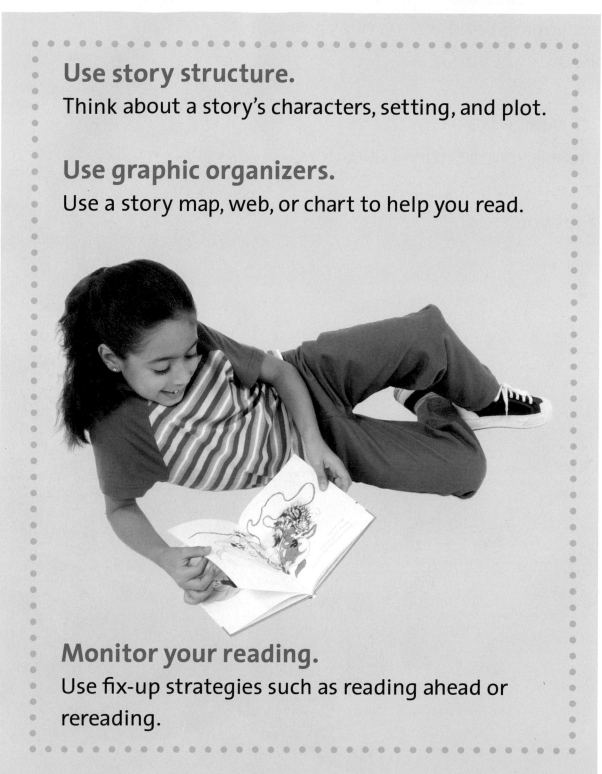

Monitor your reading.
Use fix-up strategies such as reading ahead or rereading.

Ask questions.

Ask yourself and others questions about what you read.

Answer questions.

Answer your teacher's questions to help you understand what you read.

After You Read

Summarize.

Think about the main ideas of what you read.

Make connections.

Think about how what you read is like something else.

READING-WRITING
CONNECTION

Lesson 1 ▷

Lesson 2 ▷

Theme (1) Count on Me

Hornby Train, Claude Maurice Rogers

15

Contents

Fiction

MARC BROWN

ARTHUR'S READING RACE

SOCCER

BEARS

Reading with Your Fingers

Magazine Article

Focus Skill

Characters

Every story has characters, a setting, and a plot. The **characters** are the people or animals in the story. You can tell what a character is like by reading what the character says and does.

Read these sentences from a story.

> Dana learned to read last year. Now she likes to read most about animals.

A chart can help you keep track of what a character is like. Here is what we know about Dana so far.

Dana
• learned to read last year
• likes to read about animals

Read the story below. Who are the characters? What do you know about Jacob?

The Missing Book

Jacob couldn't find his favorite book. He looked everywhere. He put his head in his hands and frowned.

Then Jacob heard his little sister say something. He peeked into her room.

Lily was reading his book. Jacob smiled. He sat down beside Lily and helped her read.

Jacob	Lily
• can't find his book	
• is sad	
•	
•	

 Try This!

Look back at the story. What do you know about Lily?

GO online www.harcourtschool.com/storytown

19

prove

sign

already

eight

police

The Library Card

On Saturday, Gus saw his friend Josie in the library.

"Hi, Josie," said Gus. "Are you checking out a book?"

"I can't. I don't have a library card," said Josie. "How much does one cost?"

"You don't have to buy one," said Gus.

LIBRARY
CARDS
ARE
FREE

"Are you sure? Can you **prove** it?" asked Josie.

"Just read the **sign**," said Gus.

"That's great! How many books can I check out?" asked Josie.

"You can check out as many as you want," said Gus. "I've **already** checked out **eight** books about cats."

"I'm going to check out books about **police** and firefighters," said Josie. "I can't wait to get my card!"

Award-Winning Author

MARC BROWN
ARTHUR'S
READING RACE

Fiction

Genre Study

Fiction is a story that is made up. Look for

- a beginning, a middle, and an end.

- made-up characters.

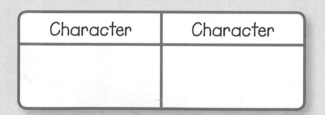

Character	Character

Comprehension Strategy

Use graphic organizers like the one above to tell what each character is like.

22

ARTHUR'S READING RACE

by
Marc Brown

Arthur learned to read in school.

Now Arthur reads everywhere!

He reads in the car.

He reads in bed.

He reads to his puppy, Pal.

Arthur even reads

to his little sister, D.W.

One day Arthur said,

"I can teach YOU to read, too."

"I already know how to read,"

said D.W.

"You do not!" said Arthur.

"Do too!" said D.W.

"Prove it," said Arthur.

"Read ten words, D.W.,

and I'll buy you an ice cream."

D.W. stuck out her hand.

"It's a deal," she said.

"Let's go!"

They raced to the park.

Arthur pointed to a sign.

"What's that say?" he asked.

"Zoo," said D.W. "Easy as pie."

"I spy three words,"
said Arthur.
"Me too," said D.W.
"Taxi, gas, milk."

Arthur stepped off the curb.

"Look out!" said D.W.

"It says Don't Walk.

You could get hit by a car."

"All right, Miss Smarty-Pants,
what's that say?" asked Arthur.

"Police," said D.W.
"And you better keep off the grass
or the police will get you."

"Bank," said D.W. "I have a bank.
I hide my money in it so you can't
find it. Bank makes eight words."

"We're almost home,"
said Arthur.
"Too bad. You only
read eight words.
No ice cream for
you today."

"Hold your horses," said D.W.

"I spy . . . ice cream.

Hot dog! I read ten words.

Let's eat!"

D.W. and Arthur ran
to the ice cream store.
Arthur bought two big cones.
Strawberry for D.W.
and chocolate for himself.
"Yummy," said D.W.

Arthur sat down.

"Sit down with me," said Arthur,

"and I'll read you my book."

"No," said D.W.

"I'll read YOU the book."

Arthur shook his head.

"I don't think so," he said.

"There are too many words

that you don't know."

D.W. laughed.

"Get up, Arthur."

"Now I can teach you two
words that you don't know,"
said D.W.
"WET PAINT!"

Think Critically

1 Who are the characters in this story? CHARACTERS

2 Why does Arthur want D.W. to read ten words? MAKE INFERENCES

3 What words does D.W. read? IMPORTANT DETAILS

4 Who do you think is a more careful reader, Arthur or D.W.? Why? DRAW CONCLUSIONS

5 **WRITE** How does D.W. prove to Arthur that she can read? Use examples from the story.

SHORT RESPONSE

Meet the Author and Illustrator

Marc Brown

When I was young, my grandmother told wonderful stories. I loved listening to them. Later, I started telling my son stories every night at his bedtime. One night the story was about an aardvark who didn't like his nose. The aardvark was named Arthur. That story became my first book, *Arthur's Nose*.

 www.harcourtschool.com/storytown

WET PAINT

MARC BROWN
ARTHUR'S
READING RACE

Learning to Read, Step by Step!

Reading with Your Fingers

from *Click*

People who can't see can still read. How? They use the Braille alphabet. In Braille, little bumps stand for each letter. By touching the bumps, a person who knows Braille can read a book or a letter from a friend.

Children at the California School for the Blind in Fremont learn to read Braille.

California School for the Blind
State Department of Education

48

Some signs you see around you every day are written using Braille letters and numbers, too. The next time you ride in an elevator, look for the Braille bumps next to the numbers of the floors.

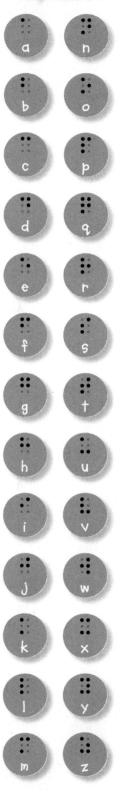

Braille Alphabet

a n
b o
c p
d q
e r
f s
g t
h u
i v
j w
k x
l y
m z

Connections

Comparing Texts

① How is reading with your fingers different from reading with your eyes? How is it the same?

② Arthur wants to teach D.W. to read. What have you tried to teach someone else to do?

③ What are some other ways people can help someone learn to read?

Phonics

Flip Books

Make a list of words that rhyme with *sat* and *sip*. Then make a flip book for each set of words. Share your books with a partner.

Fluency Practice

Read with Partners

Read the story again with two classmates. Decide who will read Arthur's lines, D.W.'s lines, and the narrator's lines. Use your voice to show how your character feels. Read a sentence again if you make a mistake.

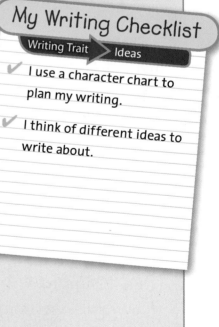

Writing

Write a Sentence

Make a character chart that shows things Arthur and D.W. learned in the story. Then write a sentence about something both Arthur and D.W. learned.

Arthur	D.W.
•	•
•	•
•	•

My Writing Checklist

Writing Trait → Ideas

✔ I use a character chart to plan my writing.

✔ I think of different ideas to write about.

Personal Narrative

In a **personal narrative**, a writer tells about something that happened in his or her life. After reading "Arthur's Reading Race," I wrote about a class trip.

Student Writing Model

<u>My Bumpy Road Trip</u>
by Roman

Bump, bump, bump. That was the sound the bus wheels made on our class's trip to a farm. I didn't like that sound, so I tried to get my mind off it. First, I sang songs with my friends. That didn't help for long. Then I ate a snack, but I could still hear the bumps. Finally, my teacher saw that I was unhappy. She sat with me. She said that with every bump she and I should take turns reading a word on a sign. We would get a point for each word. Guess what? I beat my teacher!

Writing Trait

ORGANIZATION A good personal narrative uses words such as *first, next, then,* and *finally* to tell events in order. It also uses the words *I* and *me.*

Writing Trait

IDEAS I share my ideas and feelings about what happened.

Here's how I write a personal narrative.

1. **I think of ideas for writing. I make a list of things that have happened in my life.**

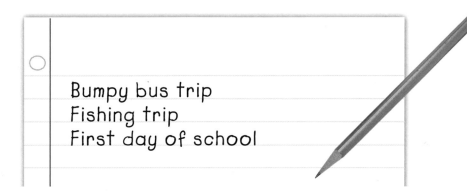

2. **I choose one idea for writing. I circle the idea I think will be most interesting to my readers.**

3. I use a graphic organizer. It helps me plan my writing.

First
The road is bumpy.
The sound bothers me.

Next
I try to take my mind off it by singing and eating.

Last
The teacher plays a word game with me. I win!

4. I write my personal narrative.

Here is a checklist I use when I write a personal narrative. You can use it when you write one, too.

Checklist for Writing a Personal Narrative

☐ My personal narrative tells about something that happened to me.

☐ My writing uses the words *I* and *me* to tell about myself.

☐ My personal narrative uses time-order words such as *first, next, then,* and *last.*

☐ It includes details I think will be interesting for my readers.

☐ It includes my thoughts and feelings.

☐ My sentences are complete.

Contents

Lesson 2

Fiction

Frog and Toad
All Year

by Arnold Lobel

D Book®

Life As a
Frog
by Victoria Parker

Nonfiction

 ## Characters

Characters are the people or animals in a story. As you read, think about what the characters say and do. Look for ways in which the characters change during the story.

Characters may be alike in some ways and different in other ways. Compare characters as you read. Use a chart like this one to help you.

Character	Character
•	•
•	•
•	•

Read this passage. How are the characters alike?

Fall Leaves

Tia and Abby like the fall better than any other season. They both like to lie in the grass and watch the leaves fall around them. Tia gathers the most colorful leaves for her scrapbook. Abby rakes the leaves into a pile and jumps in.

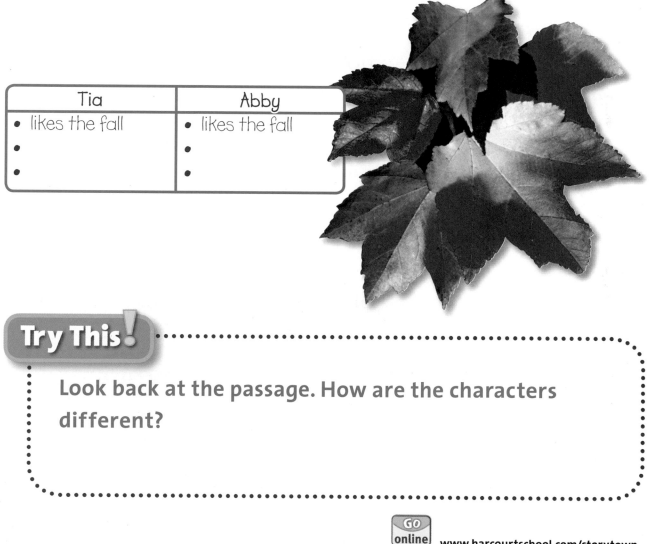

Tia	Abby
• likes the fall	• likes the fall
•	•
•	•

Try This!

Look back at the passage. How are the characters different?

GO online www.harcourtschool.com/storytown

Words to Know

covered

everything

through

woods

guess

Cat and Hen

Cat went to visit Hen. Hen was not at home. A note on the door said that Cat could wait inside. Hen's house was very messy. Cat had a good idea.

First, Cat made Hen's bed. She **covered** it with a clean blanket. Then Cat put Hen's clothes away. She swept the floor and dusted **everything** in the house.

Soon, Cat saw Hen coming home **through** the **woods**.

"Hello, Hen. Try to **guess** what I did today," said Cat.

Hen looked at her clean house. "You cleaned my messy house!" said Hen. "Now, guess what I did today."

"What?" said Cat.

"I cleaned yours!" said Hen.

Fiction

Genre Study

Fiction is a story that is made up. Look for

- a beginning, a middle, and an end.

- made-up characters who solve a problem.

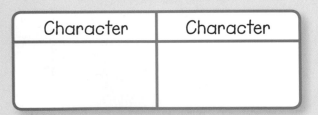

Character	Character

Comprehension Strategy

Use graphic organizers like the one above to tell what each character is like.

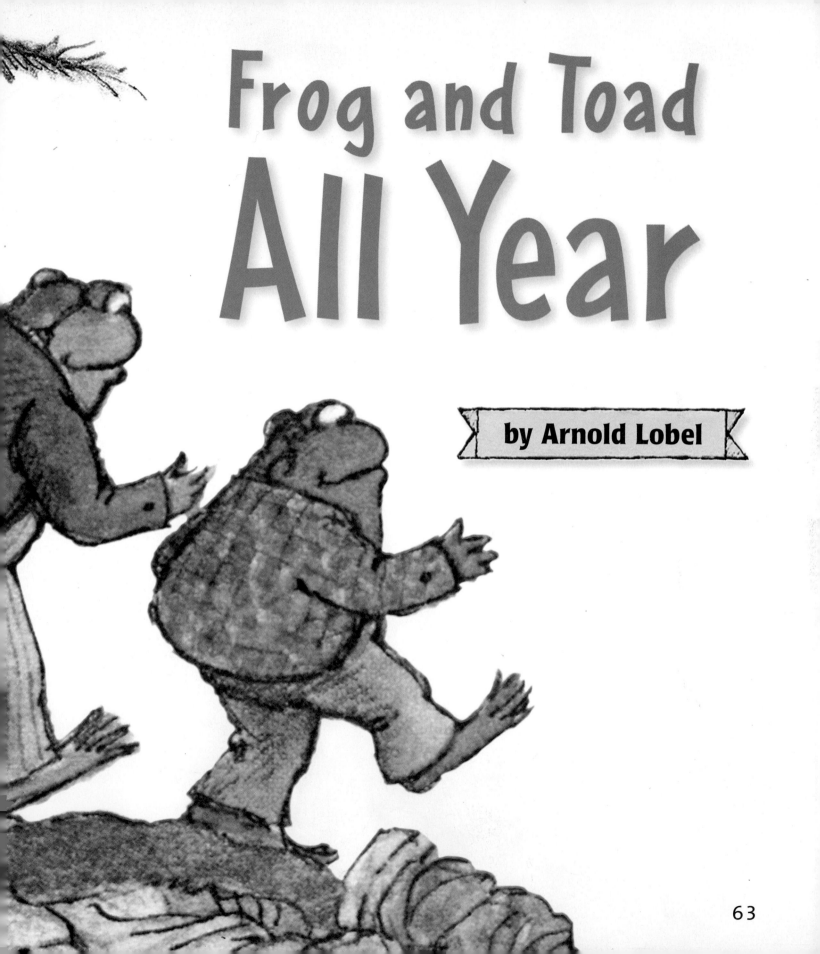

Frog and Toad All Year

by Arnold Lobel

The Surprise

It was October.

The leaves had fallen off
the trees.

They were lying on the ground.

"I will go to Toad's house,"
said Frog.
"I will rake all of the leaves
that have fallen on his lawn.
Toad will be surprised."
Frog took a rake
out of the garden shed.

Toad looked out of his window.

"These messy leaves

have covered everything," said Toad.

He took a rake out of the closet.

"I will run over to Frog's house.

I will rake all of his leaves.

Frog will be very pleased."

Frog ran through the woods
so that Toad would not see him.

Toad ran through the high grass
so that Frog would not see him.

Frog came to Toad's house.

He looked in the window.

"Good," said Frog.

"Toad is out.

He will never know

who raked his leaves."

Toad got to Frog's house.

He looked in the window.

"Good," said Toad.

"Frog is not home.

He will never guess

who raked his leaves."

Frog worked hard.

He raked the leaves into a pile.

Soon Toad's lawn was clean.

Frog picked up his rake

and started home.

Toad pushed and pulled on the rake.

He raked the leaves into a pile.

Soon there was not a single leaf

in Frog's front yard.

Toad took his rake

and started home.

A wind came.

It blew across the land.

The pile of leaves

that Frog had raked for Toad

blew everywhere.

The pile of leaves

that Toad had raked for Frog

blew everywhere.

When Frog got home,
he said, "Tomorrow I will
clean up the leaves that are
all over my own lawn.
How surprised Toad must be!"

When Toad got home,
he said, "Tomorrow I will
get to work and rake
all of my own leaves.
How surprised Frog must be!"

That night,
Frog and Toad
were both happy
when they each
turned out the light
and went to bed.

Think Critically

1 How do Frog and Toad show that they are friends?

🌀 *Focus Skill* CHARACTERS

2 What happens after Frog and Toad start home?

IMPORTANT DETAILS

3 Are Frog and Toad surprised to find leaves covering their lawns when they get home? Explain. MAKE INFERENCES

4 Why do you think Frog and Toad are happy when they each go to bed? DRAW CONCLUSIONS

5 **WRITE** In what ways are Frog and Toad alike? Use examples from the story. ✏ SHORT RESPONSE

Arnold Lobel

During the summer, Arnold Lobel's children liked to find frogs and toads around their home. Their interest in these animals gave Arnold Lobel an idea for a book. It was about two friends, Frog and Toad, who looked alike but were very different. He wrote and illustrated that book and three more about these friends.

GO online www.harcourtschool.com/storytown

78

Life As a
Frog

Nonfiction

Life as a Frog

by Victoria Parker

Look into a pond.

You might see a blob of jelly

with black dots.

The blob of jelly is full of

frog eggs.

80

Hatching

The eggs hatch.

Out come tiny tadpoles.

Growing

In a few weeks, a tadpole begins to grow legs.

The tadpole's legs grow longer.

Its tail gets shorter.

The tadpole changes into a frog.

The frog has four legs.

TADPOLE

tail

leg

82

RED-EYED
TREE FROG

A Frog's Life

Frogs live in ponds and rivers.

They spend some time on land.

They hop on their long, strong legs.

Eating

Frogs eat bugs.
They catch worms with
their sticky tongues.

Laying Eggs

The female frog lays eggs in the pond.

Inside the eggs, new tadpoles are ready to hatch.

Connections

Comparing Texts

1 Could the frogs in "Life as a Frog" do the things Frog and Toad do? Why or why not?

2 What is something you could do to help a friend?

3 What kinds of things do real frogs and toads do?

Phonics

Picture Cards

On one side of a card, write a word with short *e, o,* or *u*. Underline the vowel. Draw a picture of the word on the other side. Make several cards. Then switch cards with a partner. Read the words aloud.

cup

Fluency Practice

Read with Partners

Read the story again with two classmates. Decide who will read Frog's lines, Toad's lines, and the narrator's lines. Read a sentence again if you make a mistake. Help one another read each word correctly.

Writing

Write a Paragraph

Look back at your character charts. Choose one character to write about. Write a paragraph that tells what the character is like.

Frog	Toad
•	•
•	•
•	•

My Writing Checklist

Writing Trait ▶ Ideas

✔ I use a character chart to plan my writing.

✔ I tell what the character is like.

Contents

Lesson 3

Fiction

HENRY AND MUDGE
The
First Book

Story by Cynthia Rylant
Pictures by Suçie Stevenson

Dogs

Marchette Chute

Poetry

Phonics Skill

Words with Long Vowels

The letters **a**, **i**, **o**, and **u** can stand for a long vowel sound in words that end in silent **e**. Say the words below. Do you hear the long vowel sound in each word?

bake   dime   hole   cute

Now read these longer words.

mistake   inside   homemade   include

Point to the letter in each word that stands for the long vowel sound.

Read each sentence. Choose the word that completes it.

The _____ is high in the sky.

kite

kick

king

Dan likes to play ball _____.

gas

games

grams

GO online www.harcourtschool.com/storytown

Try This!

Read the sentence. Choose the word that completes it.

The _____ pulls the cart.

milk

mess

mule

children

finally

hundred

different

short

ears

The New Puppy

Trinda was playing outside with the **children** in her class. She was very happy because she was **finally** going to get a puppy!

Trinda had asked her mom for a puppy about a **hundred** times. This time the answer was **different**. Her mom had promised that they would pick out a puppy after school!

92

Suddenly, Trinda heard a soft cry coming from some bushes. She looked and saw a small puppy with **short** white fur and black **ears**.

Her teacher said, "I saw a sign about some puppies that need homes. This one must be looking for a home on his own!"

"I think he just found one," Trinda said with a smile.

Award-Winning Author

READY-TO-READ **2**

HENRY AND MUDGE
The First Book

Story by Cynthia Rylant
Pictures by Suçie Stevenson

Realistic Fiction

Genre Study

Realistic fiction is a story that could really happen. Look for

- characters who do things real people do.

- details that tell about the story's main idea.

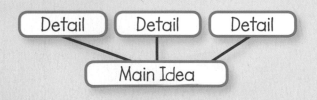

Detail   Detail   Detail

Main Idea

Comprehension Strategy

Answer questions by looking back at the story.

Henry and Mudge

by Cynthia Rylant

pictures by Suçie Stevenson

Henry had no brothers and no sisters.

"I want a brother," he told his parents.

"Sorry," they said.

Henry had no friends on his street.

"I want to live on a different street,"
he told his parents.

"Sorry," they said.

Henry had no pets at home.

"I want to have a dog," he told his parents.

"Sorry," they *almost* said.

But first they looked at their house
with no brothers and sisters.
Then they looked at their street
with no children.
Then they looked at Henry's face.

Then they looked at each other.

"Okay," they said.

"I want to hug you!" Henry told his parents.

And he did.

Henry searched for a dog.

"Not just any dog," said Henry.

"Not a short one," he said.

"Not a curly one," he said.

"And no pointed ears."

Then he found Mudge.

Mudge had floppy ears, not pointed.

And Mudge had straight fur, not curly.

But Mudge was short.

"Because he's a puppy," Henry said.

"He'll grow."

And did he ever!

He grew out of his puppy cage.

He grew out of his dog cage.

He grew out of seven collars in a row.

And when he finally stopped growing . . .

he weighed
one hundred eighty pounds,
he stood three feet tall,
and he drooled.
"I'm glad you're not short,"
Henry said.

And Mudge licked him,
then sat on him.

Think Critically

1 Why do Henry's parents decide that he can get a dog? MAIN IDEA

2 How does the author show that Mudge grows? AUTHOR'S CRAFT/IMPORTANT DETAILS

3 Why do you think it's important to Henry to have a dog that isn't short? DRAW CONCLUSIONS

4 If you were going to get a dog, what would you want it to look like? EXPRESS PERSONAL OPINIONS

5 **WRITE** How does getting Mudge solve a problem for Henry? Use examples from the story. SHORT RESPONSE

Meet the Author
Cynthia Rylant

Dear Reader,

I got the idea for my first story about Henry and Mudge from my son and a dog I knew in our neighborhood. Since then I have written many more books about these good friends.

I live with several cats and dogs. I like to take walks with my dogs. The walks help me get ideas for my stories.

Your friend,
Cynthia Rylant

Meet the Illustrator
Suçie Stevenson

Dear Reader,

I have illustrated most of the Henry and Mudge books. They are a lot of fun to draw.

I've been drawing since I was a child. I used to make birthday cards for everyone in my family. Making those cards gave me the idea to become an illustrator of children's books.

Your friend,
Suçie Stevenson

GO online www.harcourtschool.com/storytown

Poetry

Dogs

The dogs I know
Have many shapes.
For some are big and tall,
And some are long,
    And
      some
        are thin,
And some are fat and small.

And some are little bits of fluff
And have no shape at all.

Marchette Chute

109

Connections

Comparing Texts

 Which words in the poem "Dogs" describe a dog like Mudge?

 Would a dog be a good playmate? Why or why not?

❸ Why do you think some people like to own dogs?

Phonics

Rhyme Chart

Begin a chart like this one. Fill in the blanks with letters to make long vowel words. Then write as many rhyming words as you can.

b<u>a</u>k<u>e</u>	_i_e
take rake snake	
_o_e	_u_e

Fluency Practice

Timed Reading

Read the story out loud. Have a partner time you. Record your time. Then read the story again. Try to lower your time without making mistakes. Compare your two times.

Writing

Write Sentences

Write sentences that tell why Henry chose Mudge. Give examples from the story to explain how you know. Use a chart to organize your ideas.

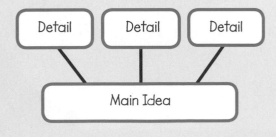

My Writing Checklist

Writing Trait ➤ Organization

✔ I use a details chart to plan my writing.

✔ I give examples of details from the story.

Contents

Nonfiction

Dogs

Animals Have Special Jobs

Magazine Article

Main Idea and Details

When you read, you will find that some sentences give **details**, or bits of information, about an idea. The most important idea of a passage is called the **main idea**.

To find the main idea, think about what the details tell you. Decide what the passage is mostly about.

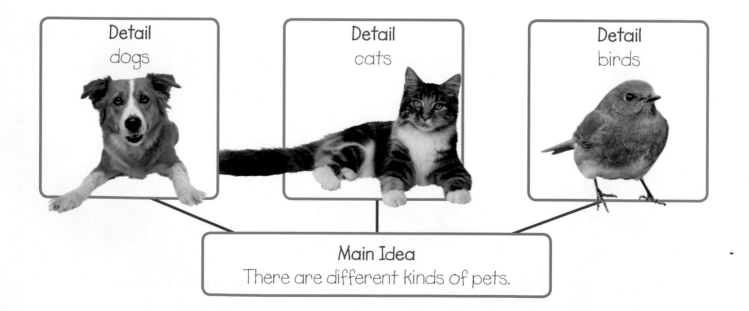

Detail
dogs

Detail
cats

Detail
birds

Main Idea
There are different kinds of pets.

Read the paragraph. Tell about the details.

Dogs That Help

Guide dogs help people who are blind move about safely. Search and rescue dogs might find a lost child. Hearing dogs help people who cannot hear. They make sure the people know about important sounds, such as smoke alarms. Dogs can be trained to help people in many ways.

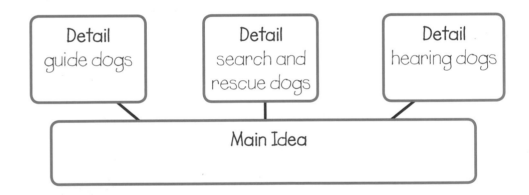

Detail
guide dogs

Detail
search and
rescue dogs

Detail
hearing dogs

Main Idea

Try This!

Look back at the paragraph. What is the main idea?

GO
online   www.harcourtschool.com/storytown

Words to Know

bicycle

sugar

special

exercise

sometimes

Caring for Goldfish

I like to ride my **bicycle** to the store with my dad. Usually we bring home milk or **sugar** or eggs. This week we brought home something **special**—two goldfish! We carried them in a plastic bag filled with water.

In some ways, fish are easier to care for than other pets. You only need to give them a pinch of fish food each day. Fish don't have to be walked as dogs do. Fish get **exercise** by swimming in their tank.

In other ways, fish are more work. Their water **sometimes** gets dirty. When it does, you need to clean their bowl. That's a big job. My dad helps me. After all, the fish are his pets, too.

 www.harcourtschool.com/storytown

Dogs

Nonfiction

Genre Study

Nonfiction gives facts about a topic. Look for

- headings that help you find information.

- main ideas and details.

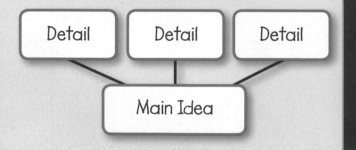

| Detail | Detail | Detail |

Main Idea

Comprehension Strategy

Answer questions by thinking about the parts of the text and putting the ideas together.

by Jennifer Blizin Gillis

What Kind of Pet Is This?

Pets are animals that live with us. Some pets are small and have feathers. My pet is big and hairy. Can you guess what kind of pet this is?

What Are Dogs?

Dogs are mammals. Mammals make milk for their babies. Dogs are cousins of wolves and coyotes. Most dogs live with people as pets.

Where Did My Dog Come From?

A mother dog had a litter of puppies. At first, the puppies could not see. The puppies stayed with their mother for eight weeks. Then I took a puppy home.

How Big Is My Dog?

At first, my dog was as small as a cat. It weighed as much as a big bag of sugar. Now my puppy is a dog. It weighs as much as a bicycle.

Where Does My Dog Live?

My dog lives in the house with us. It sleeps on a special dog bed. Sometimes my dog sleeps in my room. It may even sleep on my bed.

What Does My Dog Eat?

My dog eats canned dog food. Sometimes my dog eats dry dog food. My dog chews special bones, too. Chewing the bones helps keep its teeth strong and clean.

What Else Does My Dog Need?

My dog needs a collar and a nametag. These can help me find it if it gets lost. My dog needs a leash, too. The leash is clipped to the collar so my dog can go for a walk.

What Can I Do for My Dog?

I play with my dog every day. Playing is good exercise for dogs. I brush my dog with a special brush. This keeps its coat clean and smooth.

What Can My Dog Do?

My dog can play fetch. When I throw a ball, it brings it back. My dog can help at home. It can bring in the newspaper.

Think Critically

1 What is the main idea of the paragraph on page 126? What are the details? MAIN IDEA AND DETAILS

2 What do dogs eat? IMPORTANT DETAILS

3 How are dogs like wolves and coyotes? How are dogs different? COMPARE AND CONTRAST

4 Why do you think the author wrote "Dogs"? AUTHOR'S PURPOSE

5 **WRITE** What are some ways that you can care for a dog? Include information from the selection. SHORT RESPONSE

Meet the Author
Jennifer Blizin Gillis

When did you begin writing?

I wrote a mystery story in the third grade.
It was four pages long.

What do you like to do besides writing?

I like to read, garden, and cook.

Do you have any pets?

Yes. I have two dogs and a cat.

 www.harcourtschool.com/storytown

Animals Have Special Jobs

Animals Have Special Jobs

Many different types of animals help people. See how these animals lend a hand!

Marvelous Monkeys

Some monkeys help people who can't move their arms or legs. The monkeys do things such as getting water from the refrigerator or putting a CD in a music player.

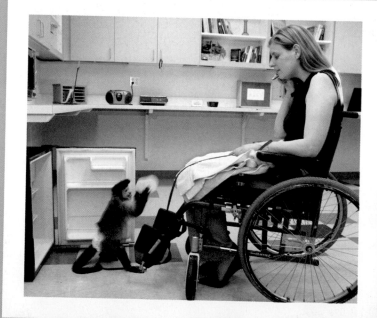

136

Reading Dogs

Some dogs help children read better. The dogs sit and listen to the children read. The dogs do not rush them or correct them.

Helpful Horses

Some people who can't see use guide horses to help them get around. Guide horses are only about 2 feet tall. That is about the size of a large dog.

137

Connections

Comparing Texts

1 How are "Dogs" and "Animals Have Special Jobs" alike? How are they different?

2 How do the pets that live with you or near you help people?

3 What else can pets do to help their owners?

Phonics

Make Sentences

Work with a partner to make a chart of words in which *ee* and *ea* stand for the long *e* sound. Write each word in the correct column. Then take turns choosing one word from each column and using the two words in one sentence.

ee	ea
meet	team
sleep	treat

138

Fluency Practice

Read with a Partner

Read "Dogs" aloud with a partner. Take turns reading one page at a time. Be sure to read the headings, too. Work on reading at an even speed. Slow down if you need to.

Writing

Write a Paragraph

Write a paragraph about your favorite kind of pet. Use a chart to help you plan your writing. Include details that tell why you like this kind of pet.

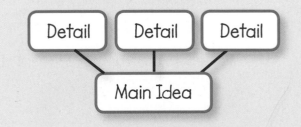

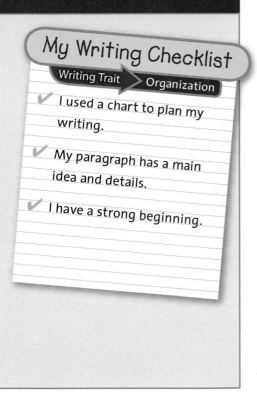

My Writing Checklist

Writing Trait → Organization

✔ I used a chart to plan my writing.

✔ My paragraph has a main idea and details.

✔ I have a strong beginning.

Contents

Lesson 5
Theme Review and Vocabulary Builder

Readers' Theater
NEWS REPORT

NEIGHBORHOOD NEWS

Grant Park

Neighborhood News

Reading for Information
NONFICTION

Friendliness

by Kristin Thoennes Keller

First Facts

141

everything

already

hundred

special

eight

finally

sometimes

prove

guess

through

Reading for Fluency

When you read a script aloud,

- take care to read the words correctly.

- try to read at the same speed as a speaker would say the lines.

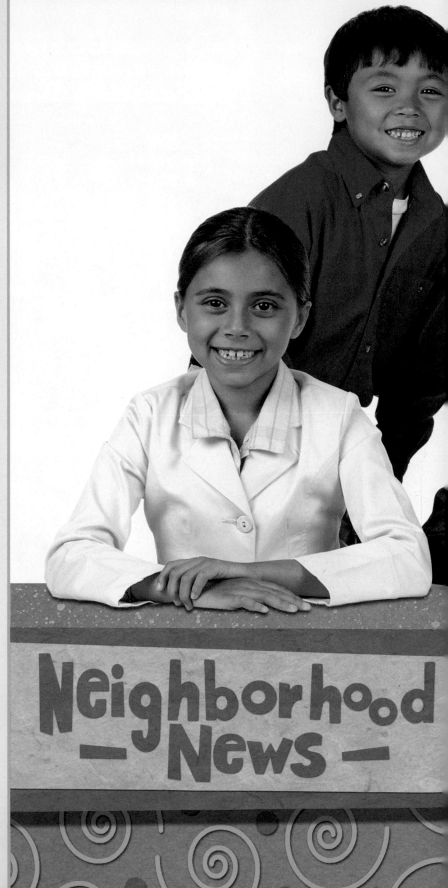

Neighborhood
News

NEIGHBORHOOD NEWS

ROLES

Producer	Librarian
Anchor 1	Sports Reporter
Anchor 2	Soccer Team
News Reporter	Weather Reporter

SETTING

Set of a television newsroom

143

Producer: Lights, action!

Anchor 1: Good morning! Welcome to Neighborhood News.

Anchor 2: We're the news program that tells you everything you need to know about where you live.

Anchor 1: Right now, we have a story from our town library. Let's go to our news reporter on the library steps.

News Reporter: The librarian has just told me the news. There will be no charges for overdue books today. Why is that?

Librarian: We want to get back all of our missing books. Then other people will be able to read them.

News Reporter: Do you think people will return their late books?

Librarian: Yes, I do. We've already gotten back more than a hundred books. People have been waiting a long time to read them.

News Reporter: That must make your readers happy.

Librarian: Yes, it does.

Anchor 1: Have you seen many people coming to the library this morning?

News Reporter: Not yet, but by lunch time, I'm sure the library will be packed. If you're looking for a book, get here soon!

Anchor 2: I have to stay here at the newsroom. If you have some time, would you please find a book for me?

News Reporter: Sorry. I have another story to report. There is a big bake sale today at the high school. I'll buy a special treat for you!

Producer: We have eight minutes to finish!

Fluency Tip

How would a person say these lines? How fast should you read them?

147

Anchor 1: That report reminds me that I have a few overdue books myself. Those library fines add up!

Anchor 2: That's why I always mark my calendar. Doing that reminds me when my books are due.

Anchor 1: Speaking of calendars, the day of the big soccer game is finally here. Let's go out to Grant Park. Our sports reporter is standing by.

Neighborhood News —

Sports Reporter: The big game is just about to begin.

Anchor 2: You've been watching the team practice. Do you think they can win?

Sports Reporter: I really do. The players have been working on their kicking skills. Sometimes they kick the ball so hard that it sails all the way down the field!

Anchor 2: How is our team feeling?

Sports Reporter: The players are right here. They can tell you themselves.

Soccer Team: We can't wait to play!

Sports Reporter: Do you think you will win?

Soccer Team: We hope so! We want to prove that we're the best.

Sports Reporter: I see some dark clouds in the sky. What will happen if it starts to rain?

Soccer Team: It won't bother us. We can still make a goal in the rain!

Anchor 1: Good luck, team.

Soccer Team: Thanks.

Anchor 1: Speaking of rain, here's our weather reporter to tell you today's weather.

Weather Reporter: I have a surprise for you. If you're going to the library or to the big game, things couldn't look better.

Anchor 2: What about the clouds in the sky?

Weather Reporter: They will be gone soon, and we should have sunny, blue skies.

Anchor 1: Our viewers will be happy to hear that news.

Weather Reporter: Yes, they will. There's no need to guess what to wear. It's going to be sunny and warm through the weekend.

Anchor 1: That's the best news I've heard all day.

Anchor 2: Me, too!

Grant Park

Neighborhood News

Anchor 1: I think that's a good way to end our program. Is there anything else you want to say?

Anchor 2: I have just one last thing. See you all tomorrow here at Neighborhood News.

Anchor 1: Yes, and have a nice day!

Producer: That's a wrap! Good job, everyone!

Fluency Tip

Think about how fast or slowly these lines should be read.

153

COMPREHENSION STRATEGIES
Review

Reading Nonfiction

Bridge to Reading for Information

Nonfiction is writing that gives facts or other true information. It uses features such as headings, photographs, and sidebars.

Read the notes on page 155. How can the features help you read nonfiction?

Review the Focus Strategies

You can also use the strategies you learned in this theme to help you read nonfiction.

Use Graphic Organizers
Use a graphic organizer to help you think about what you read.

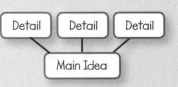

Answer Questions
Use information from the selection to answer questions.

Use comprehension strategies as you read "Friendliness" on pages 156–157.

TITLE
The title tells what the selection is about.

HEADINGS
Each smaller section has a heading that tells the topic of the section.

Friendliness

Friendliness is being kind to others and including them in your activities.

On the Playground

Dakotah is playing at the park with some friends. He notices a boy he hasn't seen before. The boy is playing alone. Dakotah asks him if he wants to play. The boy says yes. Dakotah's friendliness makes the boy feel happy.

At Your School

Being friendly helps make other people feel comfortable. Show friendliness by talking to a new student at school. Ask the new person to sit with you at lunch. Introduce him or her to your friends.

! FACT!
Smiling is a way to be friendly without saying a word.

PHOTOGRAPHS
Photographs show pictures that illustrate the text.

SIDEBARS
Sidebars give more information about a topic. Read these after you read the main text.

Read these pages from a
nonfiction book. As you read, stop and think about
how you are using comprehension strategies.

Friendliness

Friendliness is being kind to others and
including them in your activities.

On the Playground

Dakotah is playing at the park with some
friends. He notices a boy he hasn't seen before.
The boy is playing alone. Dakotah asks him if
he wants to play. The boy says yes. Dakotah's
friendliness makes the boy feel happy.

Stop and Think

How does using the graphic organizer help you read?
What answers to questions did you find in the text?

At Your School

Being friendly helps make other people feel comfortable. Show friendliness by talking to a new student at school. Ask the new person to sit with you at lunch. Introduce him or her to your friends.

! **FACT!**
Smiling is a way to be friendly without saying a word.

Today Is Monday, Eric Carle

159

Contents

Autobiography

MIA HAMM
Winners Never Quit!

Illustrations by
Carol Thompson

Two Races

retold by Eric Kimmel

Fable

Make Predictions

When you think about what will happen next, you are making a prediction. You can **make predictions** about stories you read.

To make a good prediction, use details from the story you are reading.

• Think about what has happened so far.

• Think about what the characters have said and done.

Then use what you know about real life. Think about events from your life that are like events in the story.

| Details from the Story | + | What I Know About Real Life | = | Prediction |

Read this story. Tell about the story details and what you know about real life.

The Race

Hector loves to run. Today he is running a long race. His family is watching him. Hector wants to win. He has practiced hard.

In the race, Hector is ahead of everyone. Then he trips and falls. He looks back and sees the other runners catching up to him.

Then he hears his brother yell, "Get up, Hector! Don't quit! Get up and run!"

GO online www.harcourtschool.com/storytown

Details from the Story		What I Know About Real Life		Prediction
• Hector wants to win. •	**+**	• Most runners get up when they fall. •	**=**	

Try This!

Look back at the story. Predict what will happen next.

Words to Know

The Softball Game

brother

learn

cheer

straight

caught

lose

One day Hannah asked her older **brother** Michael if she could play on his softball team.

"Sure," Michael said, "but first you have to **learn** how to catch and throw a softball. You have to learn how to hold a bat and hit a ball, too."

For weeks, Michael helped Hannah. Now Hannah was going to play her first game on a softball team. She was so happy!

"I hope we win!" said Hannah.

The game was close. Hannah's team needed one more run to win, and it was Hannah's turn to bat. She hit the ball far. Her team began to **cheer**.

Hannah ran **straight** to first base. Then the cheering stopped. The other team had **caught** the ball. Hannah was out! Her team had lost!

"Don't be sad," said Michael. "It's hard to **lose**, but at least you got to play."

GO online www.harcourtschool.com/storytown

165

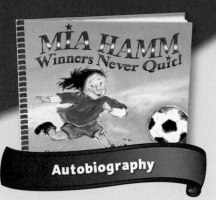

Genre Study

An **autobiography** is a person's story of his or her own life. Look for

- events in time order.

- details about the author's life.

| Story Details | + | What I Know | = | Prediction |

Comprehension Strategy

Use **prior knowledge**, or what you already know, to help you make predictions.

Winners

illustrations by
Carol Thompson

Never Quit!

by MIA HAMM

M ia loved basketball.

Mia loved baseball.

But most of all, Mia loved soccer. She played every day with her brothers and sisters.

Tap, tap, tap. Her toes kept the
ball right where she wanted it. Then, *smack!*
She'd kick the ball straight into the net. **Goal!**
Everybody on her team would cheer.

But sometimes it didn't work that way. One day, no matter how hard she tried, Mia couldn't score a goal.

The ball sailed to the left of the net.

Or to the right.

Or her sister Lovdy, the goalie, saved the ball with her hands.

No goal.

No cheering.

"Too, bad, Mia," her brother Garrett said. "Better luck next time!"

But Mia didn't want better luck next time. She wanted better luck *now*.

"I quit!"

Mia said.

"You can't quit," Lovdy said. "Then we'll only have two people on our team."

"Come on, Mia," her sister Caroline pleaded. "You always quit when you start losing."

"Just keep playing, Mia," Garrett said. "It'll be fun."

But losing wasn't fun.
Mia stomped back to
the house.

"Quitter!"

Lovdy yelled.

Mia didn't care.
She'd rather quit than lose.

173

The next day, Mia ran outside, ready to
play soccer. When she got there, the game
had already started.

"Hey," she yelled. "Why didn't you wait
for me?"

Garrett stopped playing.

"Sorry, Mia," he said. "But quitters can't play on my team."

"Yeah," said Lovdy. "If you can't learn to lose, you can't play."

Garrett passed the ball to Tiffany. Martin ran to steal it. Tiffany dashed around him and took a shot at the goal. Lovdy blocked it.

Mia just stood by
the side and watched.

The next day, Garrett picked Mia first for his team.

Mia got the ball. She dribbled down the field. Smack! She kicked the ball toward the goal.

And Lovdy caught it.

No goal.

No cheering.

"Too, bad, Mia," Garrett said. "Better luck next time."
Mia felt tears in her eyes.

"She's going to quit," whispered Lovdy. "I *knew* it."

Mia still hated losing. But she didn't hate losing as
much as she loved soccer.

"Ready to play?" asked Garrett.

Mia nodded.

Garrett grinned at her. He passed her the ball.

Mia ran down the field. **Tap, tap, tap** with her toes. The ball stayed right with her, like a friend. She got ready to kick it into the goal.

Mia kicked the ball as hard as she could.
Maybe she'd score the goal. Maybe she wouldn't.

But she was playing.
And that was more important than winning or losing . . .

. . . because winners never quit!

Think Critically

1. At the beginning of the story, why does Mia quit playing? IMPORTANT DETAILS

2. Do you think Garrett is a good brother? Why? CHARACTERS' TRAITS

3. What do you think Mia will do the next time she does not score a goal? MAKE PREDICTIONS

4. Why do you think Mia Hamm wrote this story? AUTHOR'S PURPOSE

5. WRITE What lesson does Mia learn? Use details from the story to support your answer. SHORT RESPONSE

Meet the Author

★MIA HAMM

Dear Reader,

I hope you have enjoyed reading "Winners Never Quit!" While playing soccer with my family, I learned the importance of being part of a team and how to lose gracefully. Throughout my soccer career, these lessons have helped me succeed. I have often said that there is no "me" in "Mia" because, in soccer and in life, I could never do it alone. Whatever you love to do, remember . . . winners never quit!

Your Friend,
Mia Hamm

GO online www.harcourtschool.com

Two Races
=====

Fable

Two Races

retold by Eric A. Kimmel

THE HARE AND THE TORTOISE

The Hare and the Tortoise once ran a race. Hare ran so fast that he was soon out of sight. Tortoise crept along, inch by inch.

Hare looked back. Tortoise was a dot in the distance. "Why am I running?" Hare said. "I can walk and beat Tortoise. I even have time for a nap." He lay down under a tree and went to sleep.

Tortoise kept going. He passed the spot where Hare slept.

Hare heard the animals cheering. He opened his eyes. He saw Tortoise coming to the finish line. Hare ran as fast as he could to catch up.

It was not enough. Tortoise crossed the finish line first.

"You beat me," said Hare. "How did you do it?"

"I know something important," said Tortoise. "Some can run faster than others. But if you keep going and never quit, you will always be a winner."

ANANSI AND CHEETAH

Cheetah said, "I am the fastest animal of all."
"Spiders can beat you," Anansi the Spider said.
"No way!" said Cheetah. "Let's race."
Before the race, Anansi called the spiders
together. "All spiders look alike to Cheetah," he
told them. "Cheetah cannot tell us apart. Hide
along the path of the race. When Cheetah comes
near, jump out and start running. Cheetah will
think he is racing one spider. He will not know
that he is racing all of us."

The race began. Cheetah was far ahead. Suddenly he saw another spider in front of him.

Cheetah thought the spider was Anansi. He ran faster. But there was always another spider ahead. Cheetah had to stop and rest. Anansi continued on and crossed the finish line first.

"How did you beat me?" Cheetah asked.

"The spiders beat you," Anansi said. "We always win when we work together."

Connections

Comparing Texts

1. How are Mia and Garrett like D.W. and Arthur from "Arthur's Reading Race"? How are they different?

2. Mia plays on a soccer team. What do you do or want to do on a team?

3. Why is it important not to quit when you are playing a game?

Phonics

Guess the Word

With a group, think of long *i* words that have the letters *ie* or *igh*. Write each word on a card. Mix the cards and place them face down. Then take turns drawing a card and giving clues about the word.

pie

Fluency Practice

Read with a Partner

Read the story again with a partner. Decide who will read the narrator's lines and who will read the characters' lines. Use your voice to show excitement when you read a sentence that ends with an exclamation point. Then switch parts and read the story again.

Writing

Write a Paragraph

Write a paragraph about a time when you were part of a team. Use a graphic organizer to plan your writing. Tell what your team did. Explain how you helped.

My Writing Checklist

Writing Trait ▶ Word Choice

✔ I plan my writing.

✔ I use my own words in my writing.

✔ I tell what my team and I did.

Reading-Writing Connection

Respond to a Story

Writing about what you read is called a **response**. Here is my response to "Winners Never Quit!" How would your response be different from mine?

Student Writing Model

My beginning includes the name of the story.

A good response has a beginning, middle, and end—just like a story.

<u>Mia Is a Winner!</u>
by Carla

Mia Hamm is a soccer player. In "Winners Never Quit!" she learns a good lesson. Mia is upset when she doesn't score a goal. She even quits! Then she loses her friends. No one will play with her.

I know how Mia feels. I quit a baseball game last summer when I struck out.

I felt sad about striking out. I felt sadder when no one would play with me. Like Mia, I learned a good lesson. Winners never quit!

Writing Trait

SENTENCE FLUENCY
I use short sentences and long sentences to help make my writing interesting.

Writing Trait

WORD CHOICE I use words that share my ideas and feelings.

Here's how I write a response.

1. I look back at the story I read. I think about what happened and how the characters acted.

2. I use a graphic organizer. I write my ideas about the story. I also write my thoughts and feelings about it.

Mia quit when she couldn't score a goal.

She got upset and lost friends, too.

"Winners Never Quit!"

I am sad when I strike out.

Winners learn to play fair.

3. I look at my ideas, and I decide what to write about. I make my plan for writing.

> Opening
> Tell the title of the story.
> Tell what the story is about—
> Mia, losing, learning a lesson.
>
> Middle
> Tell more about Mia.
> Give some of my ideas and
> feelings.
>
> Closing
> Write about the lesson we both
> learned—winners are good
> sports. They play fair.

4. I write my response.

Here is a checklist I use when I write a response.
You can use it when you write a response.

Checklist for Writing a Response

- ☐ I look back at the story to find information.

- ☐ My response gives the story's title.

- ☐ My response tells something about the story. It tells what happens, or it tells about the characters.

- ☐ It uses exact words to tell one or more ideas I learned from the story.

- ☐ It includes my thoughts and feelings.

- ☐ My sentences are complete. I capitalize proper nouns.

Contents

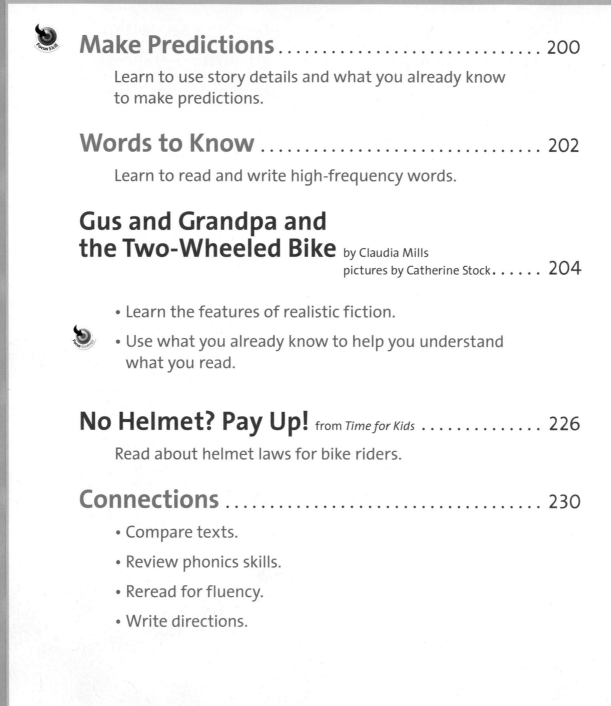

Lesson 7

Realistic Fiction

GUS and GRANDPA
and the Two-Wheeled Bike

Claudia Mills ★ Pictures by Catherine Stock

No Helmet?
Pay Up!

STOP

Magazine Article

199

Focus Skill

Make Predictions

As you read a story, you can **make predictions** about what will happen next. Use details from the story and what you know about real life.

Read the paragraph. Use the chart to make a prediction.

Lee wanted to win the Big Balloon contest. He blew until his balloon was bigger than his head. "Just a few more puffs," he thought.

Details from the Story	+	What I Know About Real Life	=	Prediction
Lee's balloon is bigger than his head.		When a balloon is filled with too much air, it pops.		Lee's balloon will pop.

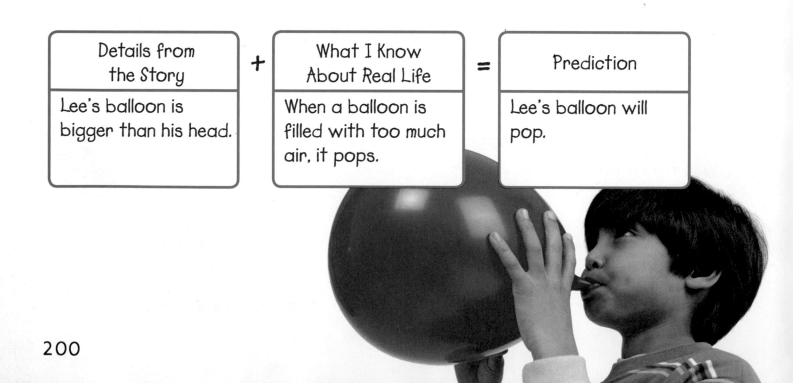

Read this story. Tell about the story details and what you know about real life.

The Drawing

Hugo looked at the picture he had just drawn. His dog looked like a blob with four sticks coming out of it. He wished he could draw as well as Luz. She could draw anything. Hugo frowned.

Luz looked at her brother. She didn't like to see him sad. "What's the matter, Hugo?" she asked gently.

"I wish I could draw a dog!" he said.

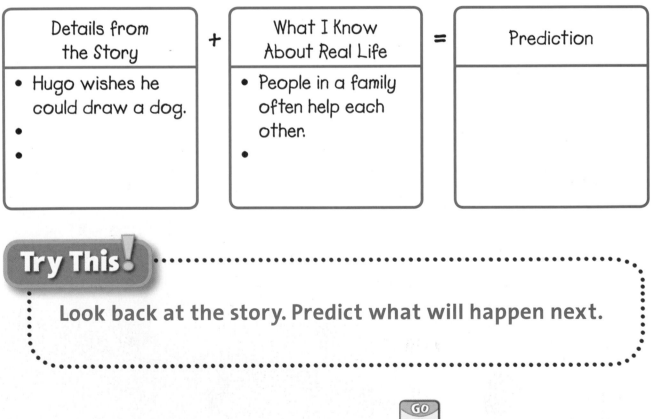

Details from the Story	+	What I Know About Real Life	=	Prediction
• Hugo wishes he could draw a dog. • •		• People in a family often help each other. •		

Try This!

Look back at the story. Predict what will happen next.

GO online www.harcourtschool.com/storytown

coming

world

curve

knee

idea

million

laughed

The Bike

"How is your bike riding **coming** along, Ray?" asked Grandma.

"Mostly it's the best thing in the **world**," said Ray.

"Mostly? When is it not the best thing?" asked Grandma.

"Sometimes I fall off my bike when I ride around a **curve**. That's how I scraped my **knee**," said Ray.

"A scraped knee hurts," said Grandma. "I have an **idea**."

Later that day, Grandma gave Ray a present. When he opened it, out fell two knee pads.

"Thanks, Grandma! Now I can zip around a **million** curves. I don't have to worry about my knees!" said Ray.

Grandma **laughed**. "Maybe you should slow down a bit, too."

 www.harcourtschool.com/storytown

Realistic Fiction

Genre Study

Realistic fiction is a story that could really happen. Look for

• characters who do things that real people do.

• story details that you know about from your own life.

Story Details **+** What I Know **=** Prediction

Comprehension Strategy

Use prior knowledge, or what you already know, to help you make predictions.

204

GUS and GRANDPA
and the Two-Wheeled Bike

by Claudia Mills

pictures by
Catherine Stock

Gus was the only kid on Maple Street
who still had training wheels on his bike.

Even Ryan Mason, who was the same
age as Gus, had a bike with five speeds
and no training wheels.

Then Gus's mother and father gave him a brand-new bike. It was as bright and shiny as Ryan Mason's, and it had no training wheels.

Gus tried to ride the new bike while his father held on to the back.

When his father let go for just a second, Gus crashed.

The Old, Old Bike

A few days and a few crashes later, Gus went to visit Grandpa at Grandpa's house.

Grandpa's dog, Skipper, jumped up to lick him. Skipper didn't mind that Gus still rode a bike with training wheels.

Gus and Skipper ran around Grandpa's yard until they were both panting.

Then Gus sat down next to Grandpa and drank some of Grandpa's homemade root beer.

"How's the bike riding coming along?" Grandpa asked.

"I can't ride that new bike," Gus said. "It keeps on crashing."

He pointed to his knees. He had a dinosaur bandage on the right knee. He had a monster bandage on the left knee.

"I have an idea," Grandpa said.

Grandpa led the way to his broken-down shed.

"I think I still have your daddy's old bike, the one he had when he was a little boy."

Grandpa pushed aside a cracked door with peeling paint. He looked behind a bunch of boxes.

"Here it is," he finally said.

The bike looked like Gus's old bike,
but even older. This was an *old*, old bike.
Its red paint was rusty. Its tires were flat.

"We'll fix it up," Grandpa said.

Gus suddenly felt hopeful. His daddy
had learned how to ride this bike long ago.
Maybe he could learn how to ride it now.

214

No Training Wheels

When the old, old bike was ready, Grandpa loaded it into the back of his car.

Gus and Grandpa and Skipper drove to an empty parking lot on the other side of the railroad tracks near Grandpa's house.

"Once you learn to ride a bike," Grandpa told Gus, "you never forget. Sometimes I can't remember what I ate for breakfast, but I always remember how to ride a bike."

Grandpa got on the old, old bike. He rode it once around the parking lot. Skipper barked. Gus laughed. Grandpa looked funny riding such a little bike.

"Now it's your turn," Grandpa said.

He held the bike while Gus climbed on. Gus started pedaling. Grandpa ran behind him, holding the back of the bike.

Gus rode around the parking lot with Grandpa a million times. They stopped so that Grandpa could rest.

Then Gus rode around the parking lot with Grandpa a million more times. And a million more.

Suddenly Gus felt the bike begin to tip.

"You can do it!" Grandpa said.

Gus pedaled faster. The bike didn't
fall over. Gus kept on pedaling.

The bike rode so smoothly that Gus felt as if he were flying. When Gus turned around a curve, his bike turned with him, like a winged horse galloping across the sky.

Gus wished Ryan Mason could see him now. There was nothing in the world as wonderful as riding a bike without training wheels. Gus knew Grandpa was right. He would never ever forget how to ride a bike.

And he would never forget that Grandpa
had taught him how. He would remember
that forever.

Think Critically

1 What happens the first time Gus tries to ride his new bike? IMPORTANT DETAILS

2 How does Gus learn to ride a bike without training wheels? SUMMARIZE

3 What do you think Gus will do when he gets home? MAKE PREDICTIONS

4 Which is better—a bike with training wheels or one without? Why? EXPRESS PERSONAL OPINIONS

5 **WRITE** How does Gus change during the story? Use details from the story to explain your answer. SHORT RESPONSE

Claudia Mills

Dear Readers,

When I was six years old, my mother gave me a blank notebook. That was the beginning of my life as a writer.

I get the ideas for my stories from things that happened to me as a child and from things that happened to my two sons.

I like to write in the morning. It's a lovely way to start the day.

Your friend,
Claudia Mills

Catherine Stock

Dear Readers,

When I was young, my mother always gave me paper and paints for my birthday. I have always loved drawing!

I have lived all over the world. I have been illustrating books for many years.

Other than drawing, I also like to read, cook, hike, and swim.

Your friend,
Catherine Stock

www.harcourtschool.com/Storytown

TIME FOR KIDS

Back to the Moon!

A spacecraft launched last week will map every ridge and crater on the moon

Magazine Article

No Helmet? Pay Up!

from *Time for Kids*

Stop! Get off that bike! Children in Florida who ride a bike without wearing a helmet might hear those words from the police. They might have to pay a fine for breaking the law! In Florida the law applies to all children under 16.

226

Why is Florida getting so tough on riders who don't wear helmets? Think of the last time you fell off your bike. Did you cut your knee? Did you hit your head?

Lots of children fall off bicycles every year, and many hurt their heads badly. Unlike a cut, hitting your head can cause problems that last for your whole life.

Helmets help. The National Safe Kids Campaign says that bike helmets lower the chances of a head injury by 85 percent.

Simon Crider, 11, knows how important a helmet can be. When he was riding his bike in Gainesville, Florida, he hit a rock and flew over the front of his bike. His head hit the road, and his helmet cracked. Luckily, it was his helmet that broke, not his head.

Still, a lot of boys and girls do not want to wear helmets. Mighk (Mike) Wilson, a bike-safety leader in Florida, says "Some children just don't think helmets are cool."

Not Simon. He thinks his helmet is plenty cool. "A helmet saved my life," he says. "Sometimes it messes up your hair, but it's worth it."

States with Helmet Laws

State helmet laws
Some counties have helmet laws
No helmet laws

Connections

Comparing Texts

1. Should Gus read "No Helmet? Pay Up!"? Why?

2. Gus wanted to learn how to ride a bike. What do you want to learn how to do?

3. Why is knowing how to ride a bike useful?

Phonics

Reading Race

Make a list of ten long *a* words that have the letters *ai* or *ay*. Switch lists with a partner. Practice reading the list several times. Then have your partner time your reading.

paint
hay
snail
clay

Fluency Practice

Read with a Partner

Read the story again with a partner. Take turns reading one page at a time. Use your voice to show excitement when you read a sentence that ends with an exclamation point.

Writing

Write Directions

Think of something you know how to do well. Write the steps for how to do it. Use a graphic organizer to plan your writing.

My Writing Checklist
Writing Trait ➤ Word Choice
✔ I use a graphic organizer to plan my writing.
✔ I use precise words.
✔ I write the steps in order.

How to Ride a Bike
1. Put on your helmet.
2. Sit on the bike.
3. Put your hands on the handlebars.
4. Put one foot on the pedal and

Contents

Lesson 8

THE GREAT BALL GAME

A MUSKOGEE STORY

RETOLD BY JOSEPH BRUCHAC
ILLUSTRATED BY SUSAN L. ROTH

The Bat

Douglas Florian

Poetry

Words with *ar*

The letters **ar** stand for the sound in *art* and *car*. Read these words. Do they have the same sound?

arm   yarn   dark   star

Now read these longer words.

artist   **starfish**   **barnyard**

Point to the letters in each word that stand for the sound you hear in *car*.

234

Read each word on the left. Tell which word on the right has the same sound.

	f**ar**m	art ant add

	b**ar**k	smell sharp store

Try This!

Read the word on the left. Which word on the right has the same sound?

c**ar**pet

still
start
stray

High-Frequency Words

ago

accept

though

clear

half

fair

The Lion and the Mouse

Long **ago**, Mouse was taking a walk when a lion caught him.

"Please let me go!" said Mouse. "If you let me go, I will help you if you ever need help."

Lion laughed. "I **accept** your offer. But I don't think a little mouse could ever help a lion."

Days later, Lion got trapped in a net.

"Help!" yelled Lion.

Mouse raced to help Lion, but Lion said, "You are too little to help!"

This didn't stop Mouse, **though**. She chewed a small hole in the net. Now it was **clear** how Mouse could help. In **half** a minute, Lion was free!

"Thank you, Mouse. It was not **fair** of me to think that a little mouse could not help a big lion," said Lion. "You are a good helper."

www.harcourtschool.com/storytown

Award Winner

THE GREAT BALL GAME
A MUSKOGEE STORY
RETOLD BY JOSEPH BRUCHAC
ILLUSTRATED BY SUSAN L. ROTH

Pourquoi Tale

Genre Study

Pourquoi tales are a kind of folktale. Look for

- a reason that something happens in nature.

- important plot events.

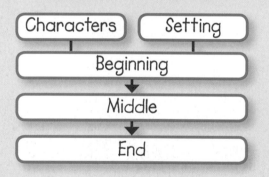

Characters   Setting

Beginning

↓

Middle

↓

End

Comprehension Strategy

Use Story Structure Think about what the characters do at the beginning, middle, and end of the story.

The Great
Ball Game

A Muskogee Story

retold by Joseph Bruchac
illustrated by Susan L. Roth

Long ago the Birds and Animals had
a great argument.
"We who have wings are better than you,"
said the Birds.

"That is not so," the Animals replied. "We who
have teeth are better."

The two sides argued back and forth. Their
quarrel went on and on, until it seemed they
would go to war because of it.

Then Crane, the leader of the Birds, and Bear, the leader of the Animals, had an idea.

"Let us have a ball game," Crane said. "The first side to score a goal will win the argument."

"This idea is good," said Bear. "The side that loses will have to accept the penalty given by the other side."

So they walked and flew to a field, and there they divided up into two teams.

On one side went all those who had wings. They were the Birds.

On the other side went those with teeth. They were the Animals.

But when the teams were formed, one creature
was left out: Bat. He had wings *and* teeth! He
flew back and forth between the two sides.

First he went to the Animals. "I have teeth," he said. "I must be on your side."

But Bear shook his head. "It would not be fair," he said. "You have wings. You must be a Bird."

So Bat flew to the other side. "Take me," he said to the Birds, "for you see I have wings."

But the Birds laughed at him. "You are too little to help us. We don't want you," they jeered.

Then Bat went back to the Animals. "Please let me join your team," he begged them. "The Birds laughed at me and would not accept me."

So Bear took pity on the little bat. "You are not very big," said Bear, "but sometimes even the small ones can help. We will accept you as an Animal, but you must hold back and let the bigger Animals play first."

Two poles were set up as the goalposts at each end
of the field. Then the game began.

Each team played hard. On the Animals' side Fox
and Deer were swift runners, and Bear cleared the way
for them as they played. Crane and Hawk, though, were
even swifter, and they stole the ball each time before
the Animals could reach their goal.

Soon it became clear that the Birds had the advantage. Whenever they got the ball, they would fly up into the air and the Animals could not reach them. The Animals guarded their goal well, but they grew tired as the sun began to set.

Just as the sun sank below the horizon,
Crane took the ball and flew toward the poles.
Bear tried to stop him, but stumbled in the dim
light and fell. It seemed as if the Birds would
surely win.

Suddenly a small dark shape flew onto the field and stole the ball from Crane just as he was about to reach the poles. It was Bat. He darted from side to side across the field, for he did not need light to find his way. None of the Birds could catch him or block him.

Holding the ball, Bat flew right between the poles at the other end! The Animals had won!

This is how Bat came to be accepted as an Animal. He was allowed to set the penalty for the Birds.

"You Birds," Bat said, "must leave this land for half of each year."

So it is that the Birds fly south each winter. . . .

And every day at dusk Bat still comes flying
to see if the Animals need him to play ball.

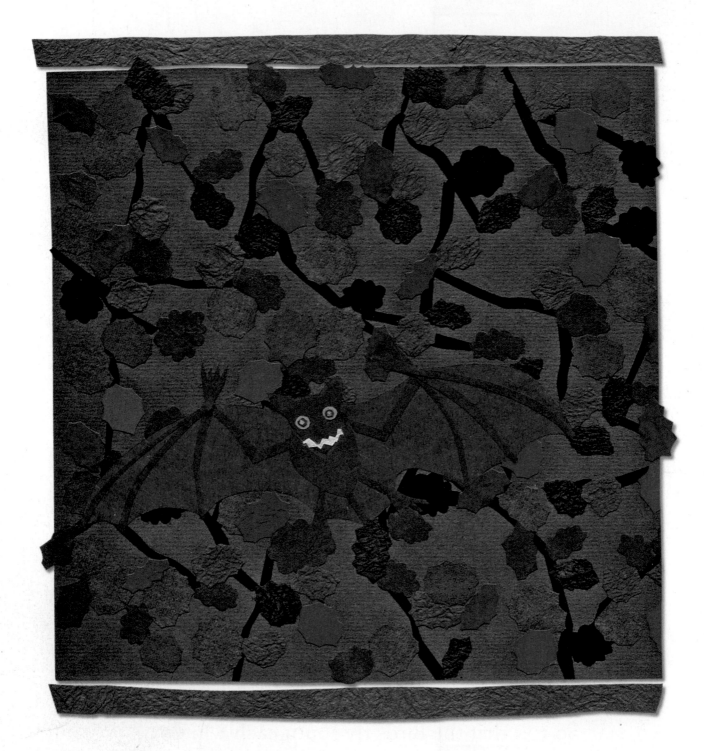

Think Critically

 1 Why do the Birds and the Animals argue? IMPORTANT DETAILS

 2 Why do the Birds have an advantage in the game? DRAW CONCLUSIONS

 3 What event in nature does this tale explain? PLOT

 4 If Bat had been on the Birds' team, how might the ending have been different? SPECULATE

 5 **WRITE** How does Bat help the Animals win? Use details from the story to explain.

SHORT RESPONSE

Meet the Author

Joseph Bruchac

Joseph Bruchac was raised by his grandparents in New York. His grandfather was an Abenaki. The Abenaki are a Native American group of the northeastern United States.

"The Great Ball Game" is a story that the author heard from a member of the Muskogee tribe. Like the animals in the story, Native Americans often settled arguments by playing a ball game instead of by fighting.

Meet the Illustrator

Susan L. Roth

Susan L. Roth made the pictures for "The Great Ball Game" from paper she collected from all over the world. She cut up the paper and pasted it to make the pictures. If you look closely at the illustrations, you can see the different kinds of paper she used.

 www.harcourtschool.com/storytown

OMNIBEASTS

animal poems and paintings by
Douglas Florian

Poetry

The Bat

The bat is batty as can be.
It sleeps all day in cave or tree,
And when the sun sets in the sky,
It rises from its rest to fly.
All night this mobile mammal mugs
A myriad of flying bugs.
And after its night out on the town,
The batty bat sleeps

Upside down.

poem and painting by
Douglas Florian

Connections

Comparing Texts

 What information about bats is the same in "The Great Ball Game" and "The Bat"?

 The Birds and the Animals play a ball game to settle their argument. What do you do to settle an argument?

 What is the real reason birds fly south each winter?

Phonics

Flash Cards

Make flash cards for words with the letters *ar*. Write a word and draw its picture on one side of a card. Write only the word on the other side. Switch cards with a partner. Can you read each other's flash cards without making a mistake?

barn

Fluency Practice

Read with Expression

Work with a group to perform a Readers' Theater for "The Great Ball Game." Choose the roles of Crane, Bear, Bat, the Birds, the Animals, and the narrator. Talk about how the characters feel and how they should sound. Practice reading your part with expression.

Writing

Write a Story

Write a story in which the characters don't agree at first. Use a story map to plan your writing.

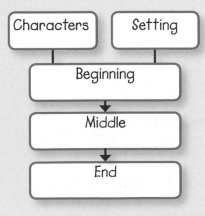

```
Characters        Setting
        |            |
       Beginning
          ↓
        Middle
          ↓
         End
```

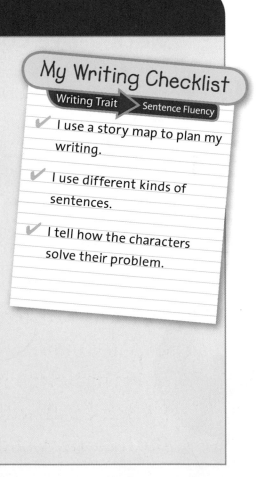

My Writing Checklist

Writing Trait → Sentence Fluency

✓ I use a story map to plan my writing.

✓ I use different kinds of sentences.

✓ I tell how the characters solve their problem.

Contents

Fiction

CLICK, CLACK, MOO
Cows That Type
by Doreen Cronin pictures by Betsy Lewin

Rock-a-Bye
Cows

Sam Curtis

Magazine Article

Focus Skill

 **Plot**

Remember that every story has characters, a setting, and a plot. The **plot** is what happens in a story.

In the beginning of most stories, the setting and characters are given. The beginning also tells the story's problem. The middle tells how the characters try to solve the problem. The end tells how they solved it. Most stories are told in the order in which events happen.

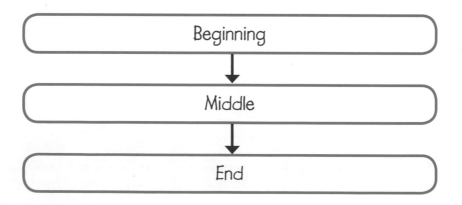

Beginning

↓

Middle

↓

End

Read the story below. Think about the plot. What is the story's problem?

Tip Types

Before dinner, Len typed an e-mail to his friend Austin. Len's dog, Tip, watched him type.

Then the doorbell rang. Len forgot to send the e-mail. He got up to answer the bell.

After dinner, Len went back to send his e-mail. Tip was at the computer, trying to type.

"Get down, Tip! Dogs can't type!" said Len. Then Len laughed. Tip pushed the button that sent the e-mail.

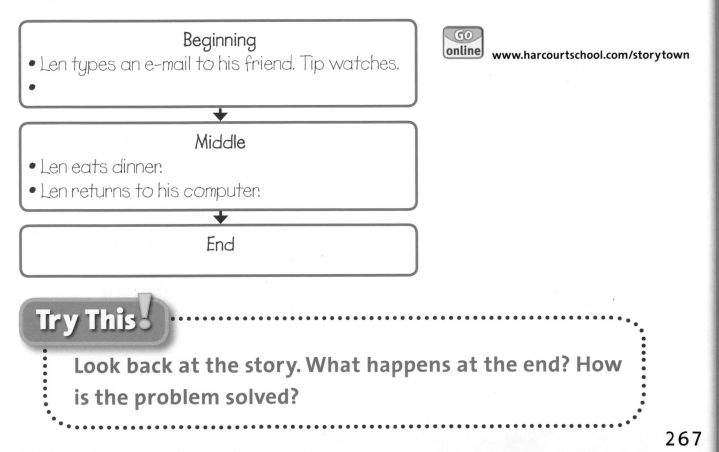

```
                Beginning
• Len types an e-mail to his friend. Tip watches.
•
                   ↓
                 Middle
• Len eats dinner.
• Len returns to his computer.
                   ↓
                  End

```

GO online   www.harcourtschool.com/storytown

Try This!

Look back at the story. What happens at the end? How is the problem solved?

believe

impossible

early

brought

enough

understand

quite

The Cat's Surprise

Lia couldn't **believe** her ears. Her cat, Effie, had just barked. "That's **impossible**," thought Lia. It's **early** in the morning. Maybe I'm dreaming."

Later Lia's friend Tara came over. Lia said, "I think Effie can bark."

"That's impossible," said Tara.

Lia **brought** Effie into the room. The cat looked at the girls and meowed.

"See! I told you cats can't bark," said Tara.

"It's bad **enough** that my cat barks. Now my friend doesn't believe me!" cried Lia.

Just then the cat barked. "Woof, woof!"

Tara's mouth fell open. "Your cat really does bark," she said. "I wonder why."

"No one can **understand** me when I meow," said Effie. "Now I see that you don't understand the barks, either. I guess I will just have to talk to you."

A talking cat! That was **quite** a surprise!

Woof, woof!

CLICK, CLACK, MOO
Cows That Type
by Doreen Cronin   pictures by Betsy Lewin

Fiction

Genre Study

Fiction is a story that is made up. Look for

- characters and a setting.

- a plot with a beginning, a middle, and an end.

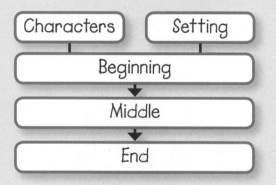

Characters	Setting
Beginning	
Middle	
End	

Comprehension Strategy

Use Story Structure Think about what happens at the beginning, middle, and end.

CLICK, CLACK, MOO
Cows That Type

by Doreen Cronin   pictures by Betsy Lewin

Farmer Brown has a problem.
His cows like to type. All day
long he hears

Click, clack, **moo.**
  Click, clack, **moo.**
Clickety, clack, **moo.**

At first, he couldn't believe his
ears. Cows that type? Impossible!

Click, clack, **moo.**
  Click, clack, **moo.**
Clickety, clack, **moo.**

Then he couldn't believe his eyes.

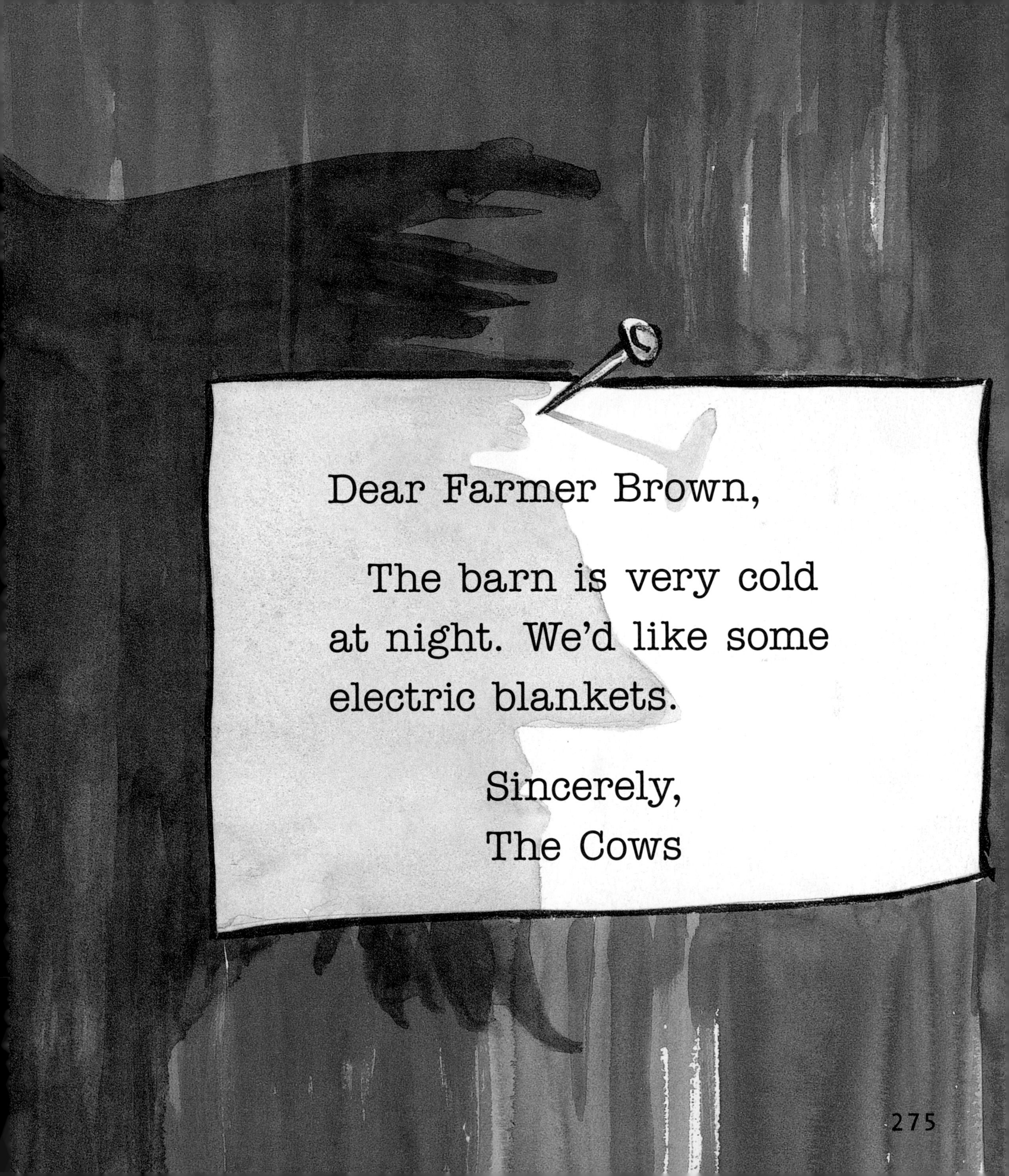

Dear Farmer Brown,

The barn is very cold
at night. We'd like some
electric blankets.

Sincerely,
The Cows

It was bad **enough** the cows had
found the old typewriter in the barn.
Now they wanted electric blankets!
"No way," said Farmer Brown. "No
electric blankets."

So the cows went on strike. They
left a note on the barn door.

Sorry.
We're closed.
No milk today.

"No milk today!" cried Farmer
Brown. In the background, he heard the
cows busy at work:

Click, clack, **moo.**
Click, clack, **moo.**
Clickety, clack, **moo.**

The next day, he got another note:

Dear Farmer Brown,

   The hens are cold too. They'd like electric blankets.

   Sincerely,
The Cows

The cows were growing impatient
with the farmer. They left a new
note on the barn door.

Closed.
No milk.
No eggs.

"No eggs!" cried Farmer Brown.
In the background he heard them.

Click, clack, **moo.**
Click, clack, **moo.**
Clickety, clack, **moo.**

"Cows that type. Hens on strike!
Whoever heard of such a thing?
How can I run a farm with no
milk and no eggs!" Farmer
Brown was furious.

Farmer Brown got out his own typewriter.

Dear Cows and Hens:

There will be no electric blankets. You are cows and hens. I demand milk and eggs.

Sincerely,
Farmer Brown

285

Duck was a neutral party, so he brought the ultimatum to the cows.

The cows held an emergency meeting. All the animals gathered around the barn to snoop, but none of them could understand Moo.

All night long, Farmer Brown waited for an answer.

Duck knocked on the door early
the next morning. He handed Farmer
Brown a note:

Dear Farmer Brown,

We will exchange our typewriter for electric blankets. Leave them outside the barn door and we will send Duck over with the typewriter.

Sincerely,
The Cows

Farmer Brown decided that this
was a good deal.

He left the blankets next to the barn door and waited for Duck to come with the typewriter.

The next morning he got a note:

Dear Farmer Brown,

The pond is quite boring.
We'd like a diving board.

Sincerely,
The Ducks

Click, clack, **quack.**
Click, clack, **quack.**
Clickety, clack, **quack.**

Think Critically

1 How do the cows use the typewriter at the beginning of the story? How do they use it at the end? 🌀 PLOT

2 How does the agreement between Farmer Brown and the cows solve Farmer Brown's problem? DRAW CONCLUSIONS

3 How do the ducks get the typewriter?

IMPORTANT DETAILS

4 How do you know that this story is fiction?

FICTION/NONFICTION

5 **WRITE** What do you think will happen next? Use details from the story to support your answer. SHORT RESPONSE

Doreen Cronin

When Doreen Cronin was growing up, her father told her funny stories that made her laugh. Years later, she woke up in the middle of the night with the idea for "Click, Clack, Moo: Cows That Type." Her own story made her laugh, just as her father's stories had long ago.

Meet the Illustrator
Betsy Lewin

Betsy Lewin is the illustrator of many books for children. She lives in New York with her husband and two cats, who don't type.

www.harcourtschool.com/storytown

Magazine Article

Rock-a-Bye Cows

by Sam Curtis

After a good night's sleep on a nice, soft mattress, Bessie is ready to get to work. The only thing is, Bessie's job is making milk. She is a cow.

The people who own her think that by putting a cow mattress in her stall, she will be more comfortable. They think this will put more milk on your table.

"A cow mattress looks like an air mattress that you would go camping with, only it is bigger," says Joe Schambow. He sells the $86 to $100 cow mattresses. "And the mattresses are filled with rubber instead of air."

Just as you have a better day at school after a good night's sleep, the idea is that the cows will have a better day at work with more comfortable beds. The people who make the mattresses say the cows feel better, eat more, make more milk, and live longer.

Mr. Schambow says stalls with mattresses usually have cows sleeping in them.

"And there are other cows waiting in line to use them," he adds.

Joe Brant, a farmer in Wisconsin, says he is sold on the idea of cow mattresses. "Since I've been using the mattresses, my cows' feet almost never hurt," he says. "And that is going to help them make more milk."

Connections

Comparing Texts

1 How are the cows on Farmer Brown's farm different from the cows in "Rock-a-Bye Cows"?

2 The cows used a typewriter to type notes. How do you write a note?

3 What are some reasons people write notes?

Phonics

Make Sentences

Work with a partner to think of words in which *oa* and *ow* stand for the long *o* sound. Write each word in a chart. Then take turns using the words in sentences. How many long *o* words can you use in one sentence?

oa	ow
goat	snow
load	bowl

Fluency Practice

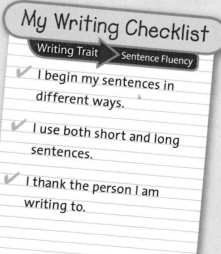

Read with a Partner

Look back at the story. Talk with a classmate about how the characters feel. Then take turns reading two pages at a time. As you read, use your voice to show how the characters feel.

Writing

Write a Thank-You Note

Imagine that you are one of the cows and you want to thank Farmer Brown. Write a thank-you note to him. Share your note with a classmate.

Dear Farmer Brown,
        I want to thank you for

My Writing Checklist

Writing Trait ▶ Sentence Fluency

✔ I begin my sentences in different ways.

✔ I use both short and long sentences.

✔ I thank the person I am writing to.

Contents

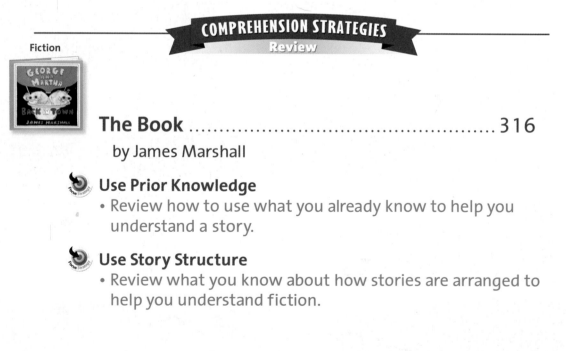

Readers' Theater
DOCUMENTARY

A Trip to the Fire Station

Reading for Meaning
FICTION

GEORGE AND MARTHA
BACK IN TOWN
JAMES MARSHALL

understand

lose

though

idea

caught

ago

coming

enough

learn

clear

Reading for Fluency

When you read a script aloud,

- read with expression.

- let your voice rise and fall as if you are talking with friends.

A Trip to the Fire Station

Roles

Narrator 1	Fire Chief
Narrator 2	Firefighter 1
Dispatcher	Firefighter 2

Setting

A fire station

Narrator 1: Many of us would like to understand more about what firefighters do and how they do it.

Narrator 2: Today we're going to learn through a visit to this fire station. We will also talk to some brave firefighters.

Narrator 1: The dispatch room of the fire station is where calls come in when there is a fire.

Narrator 2: The dispatcher answers the phone and gathers information.

Dispatcher: When a call comes in, I first find out where the fire is.

Narrator 1: The dispatcher passes along this information to the firefighters.

Dispatcher: I ask the caller to tell me about the fire and what may have caused it. Firefighters fight different kinds of fires in different ways.

dispatch room

dispatcher

Narrator 2: The fire chief is in charge of a fire station. Excuse me, Chief. Can you explain what firefighters do during a fire?

Fire Chief: The first thing a firefighter does is put on gear. We set up all of our gear so that it's easy for us to get ready in a hurry. We don't have a minute to lose.

Narrator 1: Some of the gear a firefighter wears is right here in the fire station.

Fire Chief: Firefighters wear special kinds of pants and coats.

Firefighter 1: These pants and coats won't catch on fire.

Firefighter 2: We also wear thick gloves and rubber boots to protect our hands and feet.

fire chief

turnout coat

Fluency Tip

How would a fire chief speak? Let your voice rise and fall naturally.

Fire Chief: Everyone has seen the helmets that firefighters wear. Not everyone knows why we wear them, though.

Firefighter 1: These hats are hard.

Firefighter 2: The idea is that they help protect us from falling objects.

Fire Chief: Firefighters sometimes also need to wear masks. These help them breathe. The smoke in a fire can be very dangerous.

FIRE & RESCUE

Firefighter 1: The masks are connected to air tanks.

Firefighter 2: The tanks give us air. If we were caught in a smoky room, we would need them. Without those tanks, we would not be able to breathe. Long ago, firefighters didn't have the safety gear we have today.

Fluency Tip

How do you think the firefighter might sound when giving important facts?

air tank

309

Narrator 1: You may have seen fire trucks coming through your neighborhood. These special trucks help firefighters do their job.

Fire Chief: There are different kinds of fire trucks.

Firefighter 1: A pumper truck forces water through a hose.

Firefighter 2: We connect the truck by a hose to a fire hydrant to get water. The pumps on the truck shoot out the water through another hose. The force is hard enough to reach flames in high places.

pumper
truck

Fire Chief: Another kind of truck is a ladder truck.

Firefighter 1: We climb the ladders to reach fires in tall buildings.

Firefighter 2: The ladder on this truck can reach the top of a ten-story building.

Narrator 2: Every fire truck also carries a lot of tools. Firefighters need the right tools to fight different kinds of fires.

ladder truck

Fire Chief: We store the tools on the truck. Some of the tools we use are axes, hammers, and saws.

Firefighter 1: They help us break into burning buildings.

Firefighter 2: We use ropes to get people down from high places.

Narrator 1: The fire truck also carries first-aid kits.

Fire Chief: Firefighters know how to help people who are hurt in a fire. We learn about first aid when we go to firefighter school.

Narrator 2: Firefighters do more than put out fires. They also teach people how to prevent them.

Fluency Tip

How would you read Narrator 2's line if you wanted to make others think that fire safety is important?

first-aid kit

313

Fire Chief: It's clear that teaching people about fire safety is important.

Firefighter 1: Many lives could be saved if people knew how to prevent fires.

Firefighter 2: We go to schools, homes, and stores to tell people how to prevent fires. We can't do our job well unless other people help.

Narrator 1: I agree. The best way to stop fires is to keep them from starting. That's why we all need to learn about fire safety.

Narrator 2: Learning fire–safety rules is something everyone can do. In that way, we can all work together to be firefighters.

COMPREHENSION STRATEGIES
Review

Reading Fiction

Bridge to Reading for Meaning Fiction is made-up stories that have characters, a setting, and a plot. The notes on page 317 show some of the features of fiction. How can the features help you read a story?

Review the Focus Strategies

You can also use the strategies you learned in this theme to help you read fiction.

Use Prior Knowledge
Use what you already know to help you understand what you read. Compare things you are reading about to things you already know.

Use Story Structure
Use what you know about how stories are arranged to help you understand fiction. While you read, think about the characters, the setting, and the plot.

Use comprehension strategies as you read "The Book" on pages 318–319.

TITLE
The title of the story usually gives clues to what the story will be about.

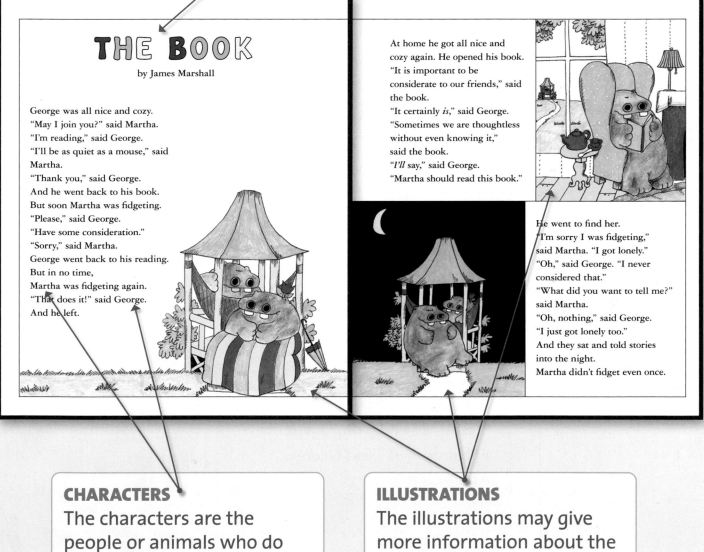

THE BOOK
by James Marshall

George was all nice and cozy.
"May I join you?" said Martha.
"I'm reading," said George.
"I'll be as quiet as a mouse," said Martha.
"Thank you," said George.
And he went back to his book.
But soon Martha was fidgeting.
"Please," said George.
"Have some consideration."
"Sorry," said Martha.
George went back to his reading.
But in no time,
Martha was fidgeting again.
"That does it!" said George.
And he left.

At home he got all nice and cozy again. He opened his book. "It is important to be considerate to our friends," said the book.
"It certainly *is*," said George.
"Sometimes we are thoughtless without even knowing it," said the book.
"*I'll* say," said George.
"Martha should read this book."

He went to find her.
"I'm sorry I was fidgeting," said Martha. "I got lonely."
"Oh," said George. "I never considered that."
"What did you want to tell me?" said Martha.
"Oh, nothing," said George.
"I just got lonely too."
And they sat and told stories into the night.
Martha didn't fidget even once.

CHARACTERS
The characters are the people or animals who do things in the story.

ILLUSTRATIONS
The illustrations may give more information about the setting, characters, and plot.

Apply the Strategies Read these pages from "The Book." As you read, stop and think about how you are using comprehension strategies.

THE BOOK

by James Marshall

George was all nice and cozy.
"May I join you?" said Martha.
"I'm reading," said George.
"I'll be as quiet as a mouse," said Martha.
"Thank you," said George.
And he went back to his book.
But soon Martha was fidgeting.
"Please," said George.
"Have some consideration."
"Sorry," said Martha.
George went back to his reading.
But in no time,
Martha was fidgeting again.
"That does it!" said George.
And he left.

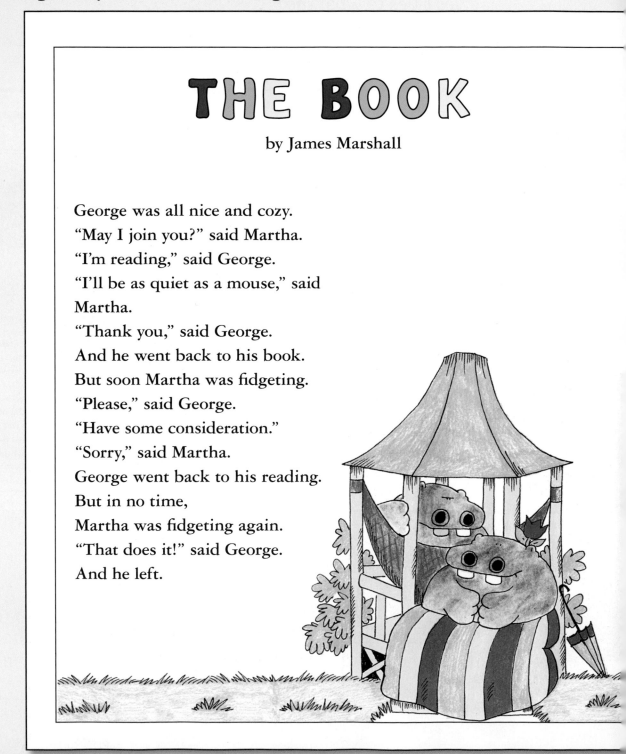

Stop and Think

Think about the story structure. How does your prior knowledge help you know how the characters feel?

At home he got all nice and cozy again. He opened his book. "It is important to be considerate to our friends," said the book.

"It certainly *is*," said George.

"Sometimes we are thoughtless without even knowing it," said the book.

"*I'll* say," said George.

"Martha should read this book."

He went to find her.

"I'm sorry I was fidgeting," said Martha. "I got lonely."

"Oh," said George. "I never considered that."

"What did you want to tell me?" said Martha.

"Oh, nothing," said George.

"I just got lonely too."

And they sat and told stories into the night.

Martha didn't fidget even once.

READING-WRITING
CONNECTION

Lesson 11	Lesson 12
Selection Titles	**Jamaica Louise James** A Lazy Thought	**At Play: Long Ago and Today** A History of Games and Toys in the United States
Comprehension Strategies	Ask Questions	Ask Questions
Focus Skills	Author's Purpose	Author's Purpose

Theme ③ Changing Times

Winter on the Grand Canal, Hou Bao Ming

321

Contents

Lesson 11

Realistic Fiction

JAMAICA LOUISE JAMES

illustrated by
Sheila White Samton

A Lazy Thought

by Eve Merriam
illustrated by Simon James

Poetry

323

Focus Skill

 ## Author's Purpose

Authors write for different purposes, or reasons. Sometimes they write to tell a story that readers will enjoy. Sometimes they write to teach facts about real things. Sometimes they write to tell what they think or feel about something.

To find an **author's purpose**, think about the kind of writing. Look at the chart.

Kind of Writing	Author's Purpose
story	to entertain
friendly letter	to send a message
book review	to give an opinion
journal entry	to tell about feelings

Can you think of an example you have read for each purpose?

Read the passage below. Tell what kind of writing it is.

Train Trip

Cody was sleepy. The train ride had been fun. He and his mother had played games and eaten in the dining car. A woman had come by, checking people's tickets. Now it was dark outside. The sound of the train racing along the tracks made Cody even sleepier. He rested his head on his mother's lap and fell asleep. His dreams were happy ones. He would be at his grandparents' home by morning!

Kind of Writing	Author's Purpose

 GO online www.harcourtschool.com/storytown

Try This!

Look back at the passage. What is the author's purpose for writing it?

Words to Know

draw

question

picture

minute

sure

worry

bought

especially

Picture of a Friend

My friend Sam loves to **draw**. I see him every day at the park.

One day, I sat down next to him. I asked him a **question**. "Will you draw a **picture** for me?"

"What do you want in your picture?" he asked.

I had to think for a **minute**. Then it came to me. "I want a picture of me," I said.

326

"Are you **sure**?" he asked.

"Yes," I said.

"What if it doesn't look exactly like you?" he asked.

"Don't **worry** about that," I said. "Just draw what you see."

When he had finished, I **bought** him a slice of pizza. He liked that a lot, **especially** the extra cheese. And I liked his picture of me!

GO online www.harcourtschool.com/storytown

JAMAICA
LOUISE
JAMES

AMY HEST

illustrated by Sheila

Realistic Fiction

Genre Study

Realistic fiction is a story with events that might happen in real life. Look for

- a beginning, a middle, and an end.

- a realistic setting.

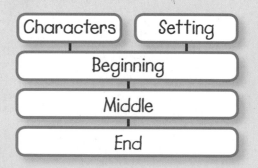

Characters	Setting
Beginning	
Middle	
End	

Comprehension Strategy

Ask questions about the story's important ideas.

JAMAICA LOUISE JAMES

by
AMY HEST

illustrated by
Sheila White Samton

I was the one with the COOL idea...

It happened last winter and the mayor put my name on a golden plaque. It's down in the subway station at 86th and Main. You can see it if you go there.

That's me. You better believe it! Want to hear my big idea?

I'll tell but you've got to listen to the whole story, not just a part of it. Mama says my stories go on . . . and on . . . Whenever I'm just at the beginning of one, she tells me, "Get to the point, Jamaica!" or "Snap to it, baby!" But I like lacing up the details, this way and that.

This story begins with me. I have a big artist pad with one hundred big pages and five colored pencils with perfect skinny points. Sometimes I set myself up on the top step of our building, where everyone can see me. Everything I see is something I want to draw.

Jamaica, age 7

At night, Mama and Grammy and I cuddle on the couch while the city quiets down. I show them every picture every night. Sometimes I tell a story as I go. Sometimes they ask a question like, Why does the man's coat have triangle pockets? Other times we don't say a word.

Now look at me on birthday #8. Grammy and Mama dance around my bed. "Open your present!" they shout. "We can't wait another minute!"

Know what they did? They bought me a real paint set—with eight little tubes of color and two paint brushes. Paint sets cost a lot, I worry. "My! My!" they say. "Are you going to spend birthday #8 WORRYING, when you can be doing something wonderful such as PAINTING THE WORLD?"

So that's when I get my BIG idea.

Now, this part of the story tells about my grammy, who leaves for work when it is still dark. Sometimes I wake up halfway when she slides out of bed. In winter she gets all layered, starting with the long-underwear layer.

She and Mama whisper in the kitchen. They drink that strong black coffee. Grammy scoops up her brown lunch bag and goes outside.

I'm scared in the night. Not Grammy. At 86th and Main she goes down . . . and down . . . into the subway station.

All day long people line up at Grammy's token booth. They give her a dollar or four quarters, and she slides a token into their hand. Then they rush off to catch the train.

Subway

Now, I like subways because the seats are hot pink and because they go very fast. But I don't like subway stations. Especially the one at 86th and Main. There are too many steep steps (fifty-six) and too many grownups who all look mad. The walls are old tile walls without any color.

When Grammy comes home, she sews and talks about
the people she sees, like Green-Hat Lady or Gentleman
with the Red Bow Tie. Mama reads and hums. But I paint,
blending all those colors until they look just right. Every
day I add a picture to my collection and every day I think
about my cool idea.

At last it's the morning of Grammy's birthday. Mama and I get up early. We get all layered and sneak outside. Mama holds my hand. I am scared but also VERY EXCITED. We swoosh along in our boots in the dark in the snow. At 86th and Main we go down . . . and down . . . fifty-six steep steps.

We don't buy a token at the token booth. We don't take a ride on the subway. What we do is hang a painting on the old tile wall. Then another. And another . . . and one more. Before you know it, that station is all filled up with color.

31 11

Surprise!

we shout when Grammy comes clomping down the steps.
She looks all around that station. "Jamaica Louise James,"
she calls, "come right here so I can give you a big hug, baby!"

So now you know the whole story. Everyone sure is in love with my subway station! You'd be surprised. People are talking to each other—some even smile. "That looks like me!" says a lady in a green hat to a gentleman with a red bow tie. Then Grammy tells everyone about Jamaica Louise James, age 8.

THAT'S ME. YOU BETTER BELIEVE IT!

Think Critically

 Why do you think the author wrote this story?
AUTHOR'S PURPOSE

 How do Jamaica's paintings change people in the story? CAUSE/EFFECT

 **How does Jamaica get ideas for her paintings?**
IMPORTANT DETAILS

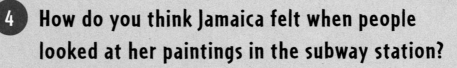 **How do you think Jamaica felt when people looked at her paintings in the subway station?**

IDENTIFY WITH CHARACTERS

 WRITE **How do you know that Jamaica cares about others? Use details from the story.**

SHORT RESPONSE

Meet the Author and Illustrator

Amy Hest

Many of Amy Hest's books are about families. As a child, she spent lots of time with her grandparents. One of her favorite things to do was to get up early to be alone with her grandfather.

Sheila White Samton

Sheila White Samton lives in New York City. She learned to use the subway system when she was about the same age as Jamaica Louise James.

www.harcourtschool.com/storytown

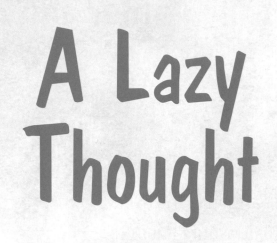

Poetry

A Lazy Thought

by Eve Merriam
illustrated by Simon James

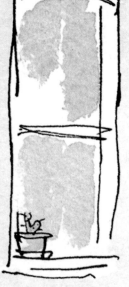

There go the grownups
To the office,
To the store.
Subway rush,
Traffic crush;
Hurry, scurry,
Worry, flurry.

No wonder
Grownups
Don't grow up
Any more.

It takes a lot
Of slow
To grow.

Connections

Comparing Texts

 Do you think Jamaica Louise would agree with the poem "A Lazy Thought"? Why or why not?

 Jamaica Louise gives a special birthday present. What special gifts would you like to give?

 What are some other ways people can make public places nicer?

Phonics

Make Sentences

Write the letters *ch*, *tch*, *sh*, and *th* at the top of a chart. With a partner, write as many words with those letters as you can. Then take turns choosing a word. Read the word aloud, and use it in a sentence.

ch	tch	sh	th
chain	patch	shut	thumb

Fluency Practice

Read with a Partner

With a partner, take turns reading the story aloud. Listen carefully to each other. Remember to add a little more stress to the most important words in each sentence.

Writing

Write a Story Paragraph

What else could Jamaica do with her artwork? Fill in a story map with another "cool idea" for Jamaica. Write a paragraph about Jamaica and her next cool idea.

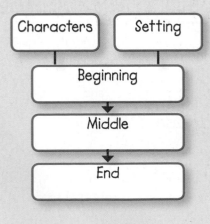

Characters — Setting

Beginning

↓

Middle

↓

End

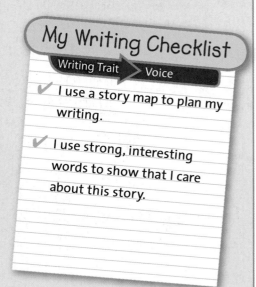

My Writing Checklist

Writing Trait ▶ Voice

✔ I use a story map to plan my writing.

✔ I use strong, interesting words to show that I care about this story.

Reading-Writing Connection

Friendly Letter

In a **friendly letter**, a writer writes to someone he or she knows. Here is a friendly letter I wrote. It has letter parts like those in some letters in "Click, Clack, Moo." I wrote it after reading "Jamaica Louise James" because I love art, too!

1732 Palma Drive
Orlando, FL 32792
December 2, 20--

Dear Tess,

    I hope you like your new home. Have you made new friends? Are you still making art? I just finished a big art project here. It is a mural like the one you and I painted on the side of our garage. My classmates and I painted it on our school's lunchroom wall. It shows us together in every season. I hope you get to see it sometime. Please visit me soon!

              Your friend,
              Lia

Writing Trait

VOICE To give my writing energy, I write about what interests me and my reader.

Writing Trait

CONVENTIONS I always proofread carefully to make sure my writing uses correct punctuation and grammar.

Here's how I write a friendly letter.

1. I choose a person to whom I would like to write. I decide why I want to write a letter.

2. I use a graphic organizer. I write my ideas about what to write.

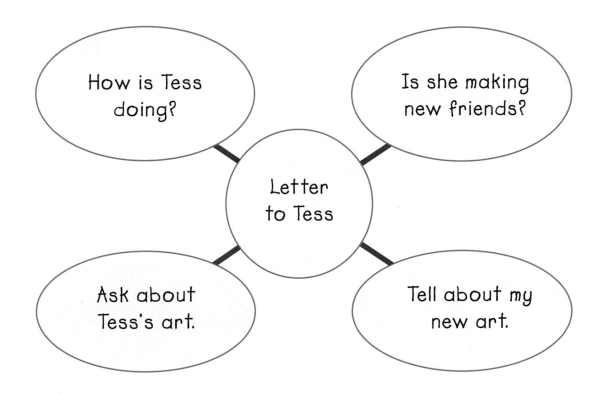

How is Tess doing?

Is she making new friends?

Letter to Tess

Ask about Tess's art.

Tell about my new art.

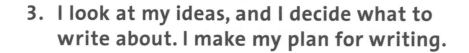

3. I look at my ideas, and I decide what to write about. I make my plan for writing.

Heading

Greeting

Body
How is Tess doing?
Is she making new friends?
Ask about Tess's art.
Tell about my new art.

Closing

Signature

4. I write my letter.

Here is a checklist I use when I write a friendly letter. You can use it when you write a friendly letter, too.

Checklist for Writing a Friendly Letter

- ☐ My letter has a heading, greeting, body, closing, and signature.

- ☐ I use my best handwriting or type carefully.

- ☐ I use my own voice and write about what interests me and my reader.

- ☐ My letter includes my thoughts and feelings.

- ☐ I use pronouns correctly.

- ☐ I write abbreviations correctly.

Contents

Lesson 12

Nonfiction

Times Change

At Play
Long Ago and Today

A History of
Games and **Toys**
in the United States

Nonfiction

359

Focus Skill

 Author's Purpose

Remember that authors write for different purposes. Authors write to entertain, to send messages, to give opinions, and to tell about their feelings. Sometimes an author writes to give facts about the world. An author may also write to tell how to do something.

Kind of Writing	Author's Purpose
research report	to give information
how-to paragraph	to tell how to do something

Bicycles

by Sonya K.

Bicycles have two wheels with rubber tires. They have a handlebar for steering, a seat, and two pedals.

Read the paragraph. What kind of writing is it?

Car Games

Games can help pass the time on a long car ride. "Car ABC" is easy and fun to play. Start with the letter *a*. The first person to see something that starts with *a* gets a point. Repeat until you have named an object for each letter of the alphabet. Some letters might be hard to find things for. Be creative!

Kind of Writing	Author's Purpose

GO online www.harcourtschool.com/storytown

Try This!

Look back at the paragraph. What is the author's purpose for writing it?

Words to Know

High-Frequency Words

imagine

favorite

board

enjoy

year

cook

popular

expensive

Special Memories

My grandparents like to tell me stories about when they were my age. Grandma asks me to **imagine** watching TV in black and white. Her **favorite** shows were funny stories about families.

Grandpa laughs when he tells me about the **board** games he played as a boy. He and Grandma still **enjoy** games with pieces that players move around the board.

Grandma says that her favorite toy was a little wooden stove. Her father made it the **year** she turned five. She and her brother would pretend to **cook** tasty meals on it.

Grandpa remembers that a lot of toys used to be handmade. That meant that many **popular** toys weren't very **expensive**. I tell him that some things have really changed!

www.harcourtschool.com/storytown

Times Change

At Play

Long Ago and Today

Genre Study

Nonfiction gives facts about a topic. Look for

- headings that help you find information.

- facts that you can compare.

Long Ago	Today

Comprehension Strategy

Ask questions that help you focus on the important ideas in a selection.

At Play
Long Ago and Today

by Lynnette R. Brent

Long Ago

Imagine that it is long ago. You have just finished listening to your favorite radio show. Now you are making your own scooter with the wheels from your old roller skates and a piece of wood your dad gave you.

Your friends are calling you from outside! It is time for you to try the scooter you have made. You run outside and meet your friends. They love the new scooter!

This is what you may have been doing if you lived many years ago. What else would you have been doing with your friends and family long ago? Let's see what Americans did to play long ago.

▼ Long ago, children made their own scooters or rented them with their friends.

Playing Sports

Long ago, children played many sports. Boys mostly played stickball, basketball, football, and field hockey. Girls mostly played tennis, golf, and croquet.

Children usually played together in their own neighborhoods. They did not have special times of the year for each sport.

▼ Stickball was played with a broomstick and a small ball.

▲ Girls and boys play baseball during spring and summer.

Today, children still play sports that were played long ago. But now, both boys and girls play many of the same sports, like basketball or tennis.

Many children play sports in community programs or for their school teams. Children play different sports at different times of the year.

▼ Central Park in New York was the first public park in the United States.

Enjoying the Park

Long ago, families enjoyed spending time together at the park. They took strolls, talked with friends, or just relaxed. They sometimes packed a picnic lunch and spent an entire afternoon at the park eating and having fun.

Today, families still enjoy spending time together at the park. Now, parks have more to offer, like slides, swings, jungle gyms, softball diamonds, or basketball courts. Many families still pack picnic lunches before they go to the park. Sometimes, they have a barbeque and cook food on a grill.

▼ Today, parks like this one are found all around the United States.

Games

Long ago, people played different kinds of games. Board games, like checkers, were a popular family activity. Marbles was a game that children liked to play with their friends. To play this game, children bounced their marbles against other marbles in a circle. They won any marbles they could knock out of the circle.

▼ Ringer and Rolley-hole were popular marble games.

Today, people still play many of the same games that were played long ago, such as checkers and marbles. But now, video games are also popular. Many children like to play video games on their televisions or on their computers. Some even have handheld video games that are so small they can be played anywhere!

▲ Children can play sports, adventure, or puzzle video games.

373

Reading

Long ago, reading was something that families did together. Usually, one person in the family read aloud while the other family members listened.

Most families owned just a few books because books were very expensive. Many towns did not have libraries. This meant families would read the same stories again and again.

▲ Reading was a favorite family pastime.

Today, families still read together. Many children read with their parents before they go to bed at night. Many people enjoy listening to books that are recorded on tape or compact disc (CD).

Today, because books cost less, families own more books than they did long ago. Also, people can get books from many places. Bookstores and libraries are popular places for people to find new books.

▼ Sometimes, family members take turns reading aloud.

375

Family Vacations

▼ Some families spent their vacations swimming or boating.

Long ago, few families took vacations. If they did, they went camping in a nearby forest or visited beaches that were close to home. There were few roads, so people could not easily travel to the places they wanted to go.

▲ Many families take vacations all over the world.

Today, more families go on vacation because traveling is easier. There are many more roads across the country. People can drive their cars to places that are far from home. Some families travel by train or by airplane. By taking cars, trains, and airplanes, families have many choices of vacation locations.

▲ Circus parades let people know the circus was in town.

Special Events

Long ago, there were many special events children looked forward to. One was the circus coming to town! Children would line the streets with their parents to see the animals and clowns walk through the town. Some towns even had carnivals. Carnivals were a place for people to ride the Ferris wheel, eat food, and play games.

Today, children enjoy some of the same events as long ago. Some children go to the circus when it comes to town. The carnival is still a place for families to have fun. Now, many children go to theme parks where fast roller coasters and merry-go-rounds are very popular.

▼ Children of all ages enjoy carnival rides.

You have seen how Americans played long ago. People played games with friends, spent long afternoons in the park, and took vacations to places near their homes.

Today, people do these things and more. Today, people can play video games on a computer or play in a water park. They can enjoy swings and slides in parks and travel to places that are far from home.

Think Critically

1 Why do you think the author wrote this selection? AUTHOR'S PURPOSE

2 Why do you think girls and boys played different sports long ago? MAKE INFERENCES

3 Why did some families long ago read the same stories again and again? IMPORTANT DETAILS

4 How have family vacations changed because traveling is easier than it used to be? SYNTHESIZE

5 **WRITE** How are the games you play the same as or different from games of long ago? Use information from the selection to support your answer. SHORT RESPONSE

Nonfiction

A History of Games and Toys in the United States

1928 Yo-Yo Pedro Flores sold the first yo-yo. *Yo-yo* means "come back" in Tagalog, a language of the Philippines.

1889 Playground Jane Addams designs the first playground. Swings and the seesaw are her ideas.

1901 Electric Train Joshua Lionel Cowen invented the electric train. It was used in store windows to show what was for sale.

1890

1910

1930

1957 Plastic Hoop Children in Australia liked to spin bamboo hoops around their waists. Richard Kerr and Arthur Melin made a plastic hoop to sell in the United States.

1972 Video Game Ralph Baer made the first video games that could be played at home. The games were only in black and white.

1952 Toy Car Jack Odell made the first pocket-sized toy car. The car was small so his daughter could take it to school with her.

1970

1950

Connections

Comparing Texts

1 How are "At Play: Long Ago and Today" and "A History of Games and Toys in the United States" alike? How are they different?

2 What do you like to play at recess?

3 What other games do children play today?

Phonics

Rhyming Words

Read each word in the box. Match each word with a picture whose name rhymes with it. Then say each rhyming pair to a partner.

very
funny
dirty
honey
donkey

Fluency Practice

Timed Reading

Read aloud a section of "At Play: Long Ago and Today." Remember to pay attention to the punctuation to know how to read the sentences. Then time yourself as you read the section aloud several times. Try to read it a little faster without mistakes each time.

Writing

Write About a Change

Think about things that were different long ago. Use a chart to list your ideas. Then choose one idea, and write a paragraph about it. Tell what has changed from long ago to today.

My Writing Checklist

Writing Trait ▶ Voice

✔ I use a chart to list topics I could write about.

✔ I write about what is interesting to me.

Long Ago	Today

Contents

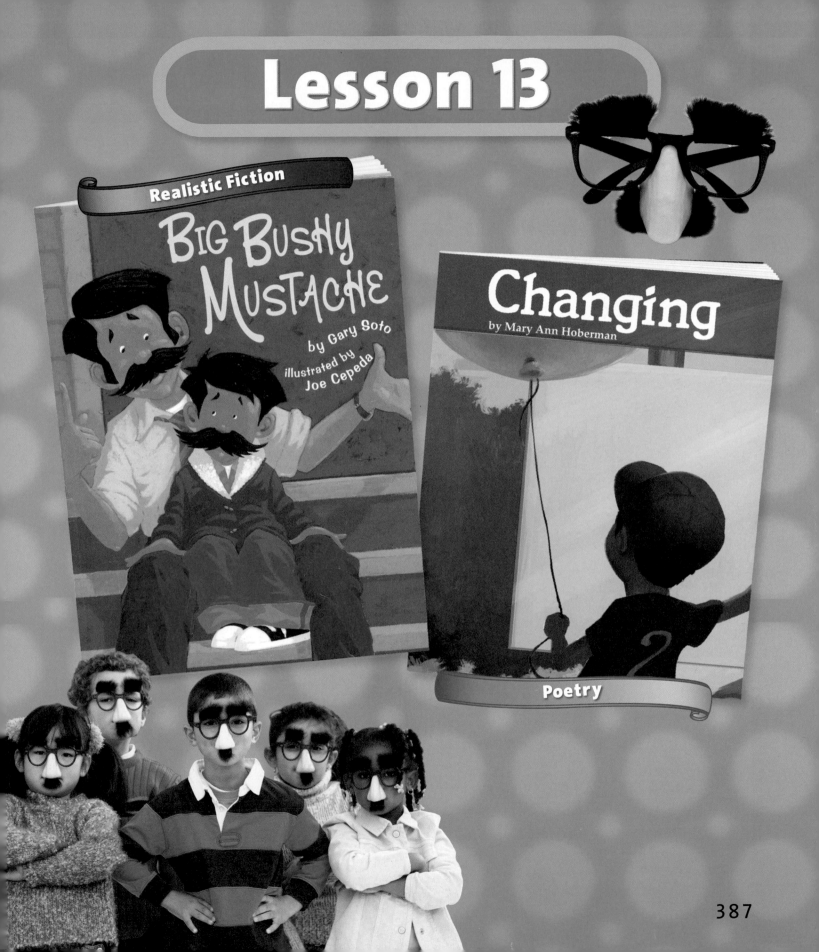

Realistic Fiction

BIG BUSHY MUSTACHE

by Gary Soto

illustrated by Joe Cepeda

Changing

by Mary Ann Hoberman

Poetry

Words with Soft *c* and Soft *g*

The letter *c* can stand for the *s* sound. The letter *g* can stand for the *j* sound. Read these words.

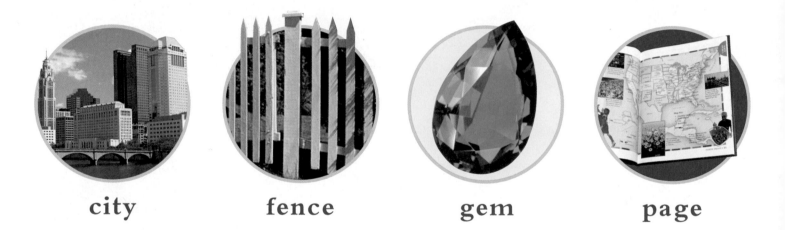

city   fence   gem   page

Now read these longer words.

center   advice   giraffe   village

Point to the letter in each word that stands for the *s* sound or the *j* sound.

Read each sentence. Tell which word has the same sound as the *c* in *city* or the *g* in *gem*.

The mice are not afraid of the cat.

Greg gave me a giant gift.

Grandma and Grandpa grow cabbage in their garden.

Try This!

Read the sentence. Which words have the same sound as the *c* in *city*?

Carly placed a slice of pie on her plate.

GO online www.harcourtschool.com/storytown

wear

tough

young

woman

above

shoes

wash

Grandma's Attic

Grandma keeps lots of old clothes in a wooden trunk in her attic. When Abby visits, she picks out clothes from the trunk to **wear**.

Abby tries on different kinds of clothes. Sometimes she wears Grandma's lacy apron and pretends to cook. Sometimes she clumps around in Grandpa's **tough** old farm boots. Sometimes she wears a silky, white scarf and dances.

Abby likes to wear clothes Grandma wore when she was a **young woman**. Abby raises her hands **above** her head and slips on a long, white gown. Then she finds a pair of white **shoes** and puts them on.

Grandma climbs the stairs to check on Abby. "My wedding dress!" says Grandma.

"It makes me feel fancy," says Abby.

"It's dusty up in this attic," says Grandma. "Let's go down and **wash** off the dust of long ago!"

 www.harcourtschool.com/storytown

BIG BUSHY MUSTACHE

by Gary Soto

illustrated by Joe Cepeda

Realistic Fiction

Genre Study

Realistic fiction is a story that could really happen. Look for

- characters who do things that real people do.
- a realistic plot.

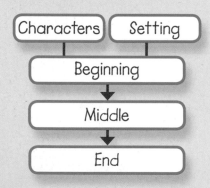

Characters	Setting

Beginning

↓

Middle

↓

End

Comprehension Strategy

Monitor comprehension—Reread if you do not understand something.

392

Big Bushy Mustache

by Gary Soto

illustrated by Joe Cepeda

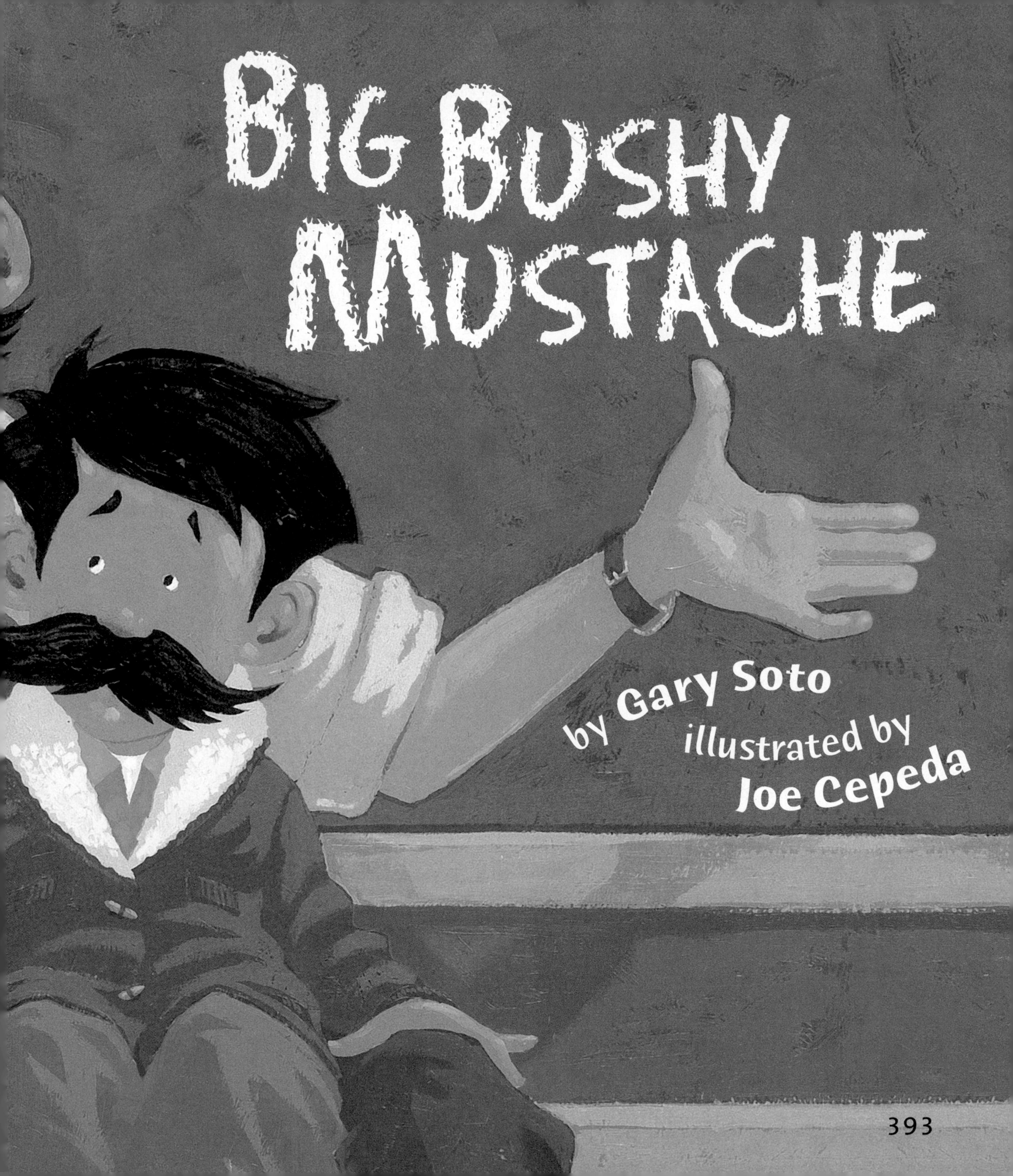

People always said Ricky looked just like his mother.

"He has beautiful eyes, exactly like yours, Rosa!" said Mrs. Sanchez, the crossing guard, as his mother took him to school one morning.

"Thanks!" Ricky's mother shouted, and turned a big smile on him. "Have a good day, *mi'jo.*" Then she gave him a kiss.

Ricky went into school frowning. He was a boy. Why didn't people say he looked like his father?

That morning his teacher, Mrs. Cortez, brought out a large box from the closet and set it on her desk. She took out a hat and a *sarape.* She took out a sword and raised it toward the ceiling.

"Class, for our next unit we're going to do a play about *Cinco de Mayo.* That's a holiday that celebrates the Mexican victory over the French army."

Mrs. Cortez looked around the room. Her eyes settled on Ricky. "Ricky, do you want to carry the sword?"

Ricky shook his head no.

"Do you want to wear this white shirt?" she asked.

Again Ricky shook his head no. And he shook his head to the sombrero, the captain's hat, the purple cape, the tiny Mexican flag.

But when Mrs. Cortez took out a big, bushy mustache, something clicked. This time Ricky nodded yes.

For the rest of the day, the class practiced their parts.
Some of the children played Mexican soldiers. Some of the
children played French soldiers.

All the while, Ricky played with his mustache. It tickled
his lip. It made him feel tough.

When school was over, Mrs. Cortez told the class to
leave the costumes in their desks.

Ricky took off his mustache. But instead of leaving it behind, he put it in his pocket. He wanted to take it home. He wanted to surprise his father when he got home from work.

Maybe Mami will take a picture of us, he thought. *We could stand next to each other in front of our new car.*

After Ricky left the school, he pressed the mustache back onto his lip. He felt grown-up.

A man on the street called out, "Hello, soldier."

Ricky passed a woman carrying groceries. She said, "What a handsome young man."

He passed a kindergartner, who said, "Mister, would you help me tie my shoes?"

Ricky laughed and ran home. He climbed the wooden
steps, pushed open the door, and rushed into the kitchen,
where his mother was peeling apples.

"*¡Hola, Mami!*" he said. "I'm hungry."

He looked up and waited for her to say something about
his big, bushy mustache.

But she only smiled and handed him a slice of apple.

"*Mi'jo*, wash your hands and help me with the apples," she said.

Ricky's smile disappeared. Didn't she notice?

"Look, Mami. Isn't my *bigote* great?" he said, tugging at her apron.

His mother looked at him.

"*¿Bigote?* What are you talking about?"

"This one," he said. He touched his lip, but the mustache was gone! He felt around his face. It was not on his cheek. It was not on his chin. He looked down to the floor, but it wasn't there, either.

I must have lost it on the way home, Ricky thought. Without saying anything, he ran out the front door.

He retraced his steps, eyes wide open. He dug through a pile of raked leaves. He parted the tall grass that grew along a fence. He looked in the street, between parked cars, and in flower beds.

He jumped with hope when he saw a black thing. But when he bent over to pick it up, he discovered that it was a squashed crayon.

Ricky sat on the curb and cried. The mustache was gone.

When he got home, Ricky told his mother what had happened. She wiped her hands on a dish towel and hugged him.

At dinner, he wanted to tell Papi too, but the words would not come out. They were stuck in his throat.

He watched his father's big, bushy mustache move up and down when he chewed.

Under his breath, Ricky whispered, "Mustache," but his father didn't hear. He talked about his work.

After dinner, Ricky went to his bedroom. With a black crayon, he colored a sheet of paper and then cut it into the shape of a mustache. He taped it to his mouth and stood before the mirror. But it didn't look real. He tore it off, crumpled it, and tossed it on the floor.

In the closet, Ricky found a can of black shoe polish. He looked in the mirror and smeared a line above his lip, but it was too flat, not thick and bushy at all.

Finally, he dug out a pair of old shoes. The strings were black. He cut them in short strips and bound them together with a rubber band. He held the creation above his lip. It looked like a black mop. And smelled like old socks.

That night, after he put on his pajamas, Ricky went into the living room, where his father was listening to the radio.

"Papi, I lost my mustache . . . *mi bigote.*"

His father laughed. "What mustache?"

Ricky climbed into his father's lap and told him everything. His father smiled and told him a story about a hen that tried to become a swan. It was a good story, but it still didn't solve his problem. Tomorrow he would have to face Mrs. Cortez.

The next morning, Ricky got out of bed slowly. He dressed slowly. He combed his hair slowly. At breakfast, he chewed his cereal slowly. He raised his eyes slowly when his father came into the kitchen. "*Buenos días,*" he greeted Ricky.

Then Ricky's mother came into the kitchen. "*Mi'jo,* I have a surprise for you," she said.

Mami held out a closed fist and let it open like a flower. Sitting in her palm was a mustache. It was big and bushy.

"You found it!" Ricky shouted happily.

"Well, yes and no," Mami said as she poured herself a cup of coffee.

Ricky pressed the new mustache to his lip. He ate his cereal, and the mustache moved up and down, just like his father's.

But something was different about his father's smile. His lip looked funny. Ricky jumped up and threw his arms around Papi's neck.

"*Gracias*, Papi! Thank you!" he cried.

"That's okay," Papi told him. "But next time listen to your teacher."

Then Papi touched his son's hair softly. "And, hey, now I look just like you!"

Ricky grinned a mile wide.

When Ricky walked to school, he carried the mustache not on his lip, but safely in his pocket.

It wasn't just a bushy disguise anymore, but a gift from his papi.

Think Critically

1 Is "Big Bushy Mustache" fiction or nonfiction? How do you know? FICTION AND NONFICTION

2 How do Ricky's feelings change from the beginning of the story to the middle of the story? CHARACTERS' EMOTIONS

3 Why does the author include Spanish words in the story? AUTHOR'S CRAFT/WORD CHOICE

4 Why do you think Ricky will be more careful with his father's gift than with the mustache his teacher gave him? MAKE INFERENCES

5 **WRITE** Do you think Ricky will listen to his teacher next time? Use details from the story to explain your answer. SHORT RESPONSE

Meet the Author

Gary Soto

Dear Reader,

When I write stories, I often use the neighborhood where I grew up to get ideas. Sometimes I even use my own family members as characters!

One of my favorite things to do is read. I also enjoy tennis, theater, basketball, traveling, and sometimes working in the garden.

Your friend,
Gary Soto

 www.harcourtschool.com/storytown

Meet the Illustrator

Dear Reader,

When I illustrate stories, I read the story many times first. Then I draw the place where the story happens. I draw the people last.

I like to include inside jokes in all of my pictures. I often include my family in the background. Can you find my family?

Your friend,
Joe Cepeda

417

Changing

by Mary Ann Hoberman

I know what I feel like;
I'd like to be *you*
And feel what *you* feel like
And do what *you* do.
I'd like to change places
For maybe a week
And look like your look-like
And speak as you speak
And think what you're thinking
And go where you go
And feel what you're feeling
And know what you know.
I wish we could do it;
What fun it would be
If I could try you out
And you could try me.

Connections

Comparing Texts

 1 How are Ricky and the boy in the poem "Changing" alike?

 2 What costumes do you like to wear?

 3 What are some ways people can change the way they look?

Phonics

Make a Match

On one index card, write two words in which *c* has the soft sound. On another card, write two words in which *g* has the soft sound. Switch cards with a partner. Take turns naming rhyming words for the words on the cards.

trace
ice

edge
rage

Fluency Practice

Read with a Partner

Take turns reading the story again with a partner. As a reader, work on keeping groups of words together. If you make a mistake, go back and reread. As a listener, follow along and help the reader with hard words. Switch roles after every page.

Writing

Write About a Story

Write about the different mustaches Ricky makes. Look back at the story and your story map for details about each mustache. Use the details to help you write your sentences.

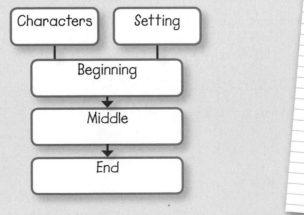

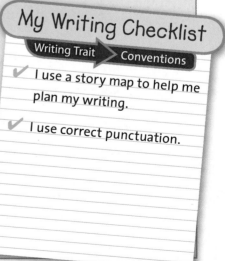

My Writing Checklist

Writing Trait ▶ Conventions

✔ I use a story map to help me plan my writing.

✔ I use correct punctuation.

Contents

Lesson 14

Nonfiction

Rain Forest Babies

by Kathy Darling

Scholastic 0-590-97440-8

Tapir
Baby Tapir is Born!

HOUSTON
ZOO
NATURALLY
WILD

Website

423

Focus Skill

Fiction and Nonfiction

There are two main kinds of writing—fiction and nonfiction. **Fiction** is about made-up events and characters. A fiction writer wants to tell a story for you to enjoy. **Nonfiction** is about real events and real people or animals. A nonfiction writer wants to give you information.

Fiction	Nonfiction
made-up events	real events
made-up characters	real people or animals

Read the paragraph. What kind of writing is it? How can you tell?

Tropical Trip

President Theodore Roosevelt set sail for South America on October 4, 1913. He was on a trip to learn about jungles in Brazil. For two months, he explored a river that flowed through the rain forest. President Roosevelt traveled in canoes with his son, Kermit, and about twenty other people.

Fiction	Nonfiction

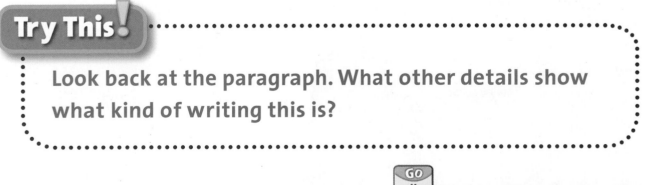

Try This!

Look back at the paragraph. What other details show what kind of writing this is?

GO online   www.harcourtschool.com/storytown

Words to Know

interesting

father

touch

thumb

sweat

care

November 15

Dear Kayla,

I took an **interesting** trip last month. My **father** took me with him on a research trip to a rain forest. He said I would see, hear, smell, taste, and **touch** some amazing things in the rain forest. He was right!

My dad studies the plants that grow in rain forests. He's good with plants. My mom says he has a green **thumb**.

426

We flew to the Amazon rain forest in South America. This is the largest rain forest in the world! I was covered with **sweat** the whole time I was there. That's because the rain forest is warm and wet all year.

I learned on this trip that we need to take **care** of the rain forests. Did you know that more than half of the world's plants and animals live in rain forests?

Your friend,

David

www.harcourtschool.com/storytown

Rain Forest Babies

Nonfiction

Genre Study

Nonfiction gives facts about a topic. Look for

- main ideas in paragraphs.

- facts about subjects you want to learn more about.

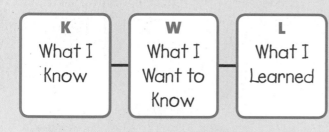

K	W	L
What I Know	What I Want to Know	What I Learned

Comprehension Strategy

Focus Strategy

Monitor Comprehension—Reread a section if something does not make sense to you.

RAIN

FOREST BABIES

BY KATHY DARLING

Tropical Rain Forests

The rain forests are Earth's giant nursery. You can find new babies at any time of the year.

Half of all living things on the planet are found in the rain forests. All the tropical rain forests are alike: hot, wet, and green. But each one has animals and plants that belong to it alone.

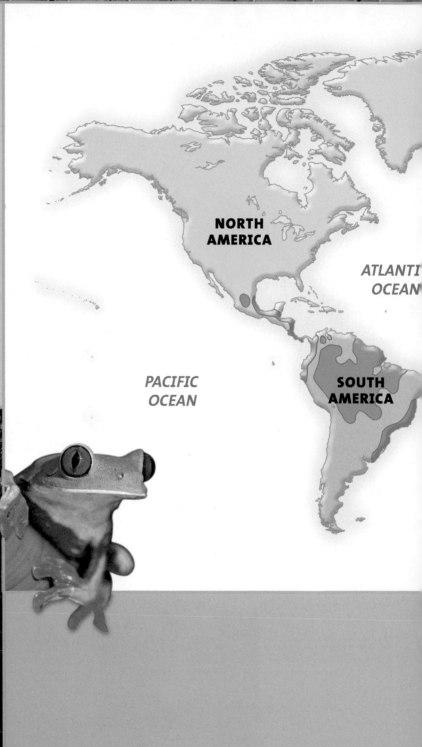

NORTH AMERICA

ATLANTI OCEAN

PACIFIC OCEAN

SOUTH AMERICA

of the World

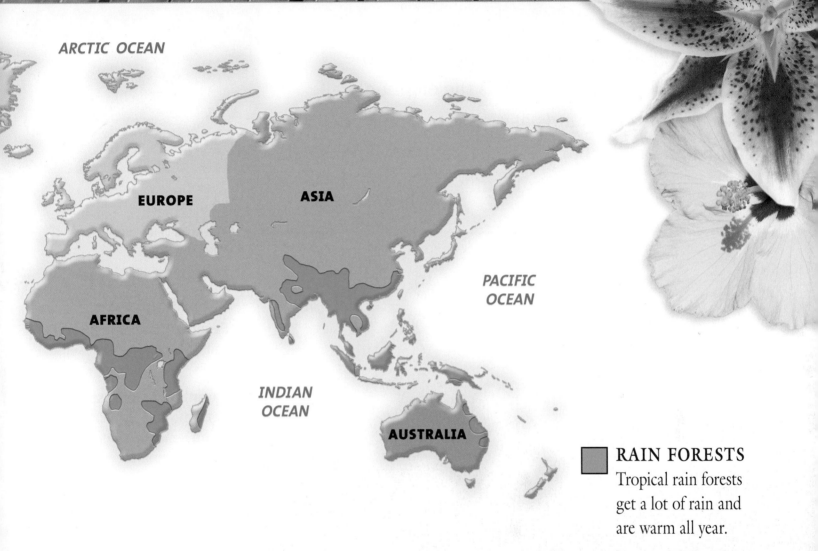

ARCTIC OCEAN

EUROPE

ASIA

AFRICA

PACIFIC
OCEAN

INDIAN
OCEAN

AUSTRALIA

RAIN FORESTS
Tropical rain forests
get a lot of rain and
are warm all year.

Come and see what is hatching from
the eggs and peeking out of the nests. The
rain forests are home to some of the most
interesting babies you will ever meet.

Elephant

The biggest animal in the rain forest is the elephant. The biggest baby is the elephant calf. Three hundred pounds at birth, it will become a thousand-pound baby in less than two years. That elephant milk is powerful stuff!

Elephant
(Sumatran Elephant)

- **Baby name:** Calf
- **Birth weight:** 300 pounds
- **Favorite food:** Babies drink milk; adults eat leaves and grass.
- **Parent care:** Baby stays with mother for 10 or more years in a herd of related females.

The elephant baby sucks on its trunk just as a human baby sucks on its thumb. Trunks are good for other things too: sniffing, putting food and water into the mouth, and playing with sticks and leaves. This calf is part of a big family called a *herd*. There are lots of other elephant babies in the herd, but this calf is only two weeks old and still too little to play with the other babies.

433

Tiger

This cute little tiger cub will grow up to be a hundred times bigger than the kitty in your house. It will do a lot of the same things a house cat does, but it will not be able to purr.

Tiger
(Bengal Tiger)

- **Baby name:** Cub
- **Birth weight:** 2 pounds
- **Favorite food:** Babies drink milk; adults eat meat.
- **Parent care:** Cubs stay with mother for 2 years. Father does not help.

The tiger is one of the "four who can roar."
Three of the roaring cats—the tigers, the
leopards, and the jaguars—live in rain forests.
Lions, the fourth roarer, sometimes live in
forests, but never in rain forests.

Macaw

Mother and father macaw have the most beautiful feathers in the forest. But their chicks have none at all. Only for a few days, though. Then fluffy "baby feathers" called *down* cover their wrinkly skin. This two-week-old Hahn's macaw (right) is warm in its down coat, but it can't fly with this kind of feather. Down is not waterproof, either, so the baby macaw won't go far from the nest hole.

Macaw
(Hahn's Macaw,
Blue and Gold Macaw)

- **Baby name:** Chick, called a fledgling when it can fly

- **Birth weight:** 1 ounce

- **Favorite food:** Partly digested fruit and seeds brought by parents

- **Parent care:** Both mother and father feed, protect, and teach the babies for 2 or 3 years.

At nine weeks, a blue and gold macaw baby already has most of the bright, strong feathers it will need to fly away. But the fledgling is in no hurry to leave its loving parents. Young macaws stay with their family for two or three years.

Frog

Look, but don't touch! People who live in the rain forest know to keep away from these beautiful baby frogs. The golden froglets are small, but they are able to take care of themselves. If danger comes, a poison oozes out of their skin. This "sweat" is very deadly.

Frog
(Poison Arrow Frog)

- **Baby name:** Tadpole when young, froglet when older
- **Birth size:** No bigger than a raisin
- **Favorite food:** Insects, ants, tiny water animals
- **Parent care:** Tadpoles are fed by both parents.

438

Bright gold is one of the warning colors that poison frogs use. Here are some of the bright patterns they use to say, *Danger! Keep away.*

Kangaroo

Surprise! There are kangaroos in rain forests. These red-legged pademelons live on the ground. Other kinds hop around in the treetops.

All baby kangaroos have the same name. When they are carried in Mother's pouch, both boy and girl babies are called *joey.*

Kangaroo
(Red-legged Pademelon)

- **Baby name:** Joey
- **Birth weight:** About the same as a grain of rice
- **Favorite food:** Babies drink milk; adults eat leaves and grass.
- **Parent care:** Mother carries baby in pouch. Father does not help.

This little one is too big for the pouch, but it will keep close to its mother's side for protection. Don't let Mom's sweet face fool you. She can deliver a kick that would make a karate champion proud.

Sugar Glider

The sugar glider jumps out of trees. Without a parachute . . . and at night. Its target is not the ground but a nearby tree. It leaps from tree to tree to get the sweet sap.

Sugar Glider
(Lesser Sugar Glider)

- **Birth weight:** Less than a grain of rice

- **Favorite food:** Babies drink only milk for the first 100 days; adults prefer tree sap and insects.

- **Parent care:** Mother keeps babies in pouch for 70 days and then feeds them in nest for another month. Although gliders live in a colony and share a nest, the mother does all the child-raising chores.

442

Although it looks like a flying squirrel, the sugar glider is not even a close relative. It is a marsupial—an animal with a pouch. Only as big as a mouse, this baby, four weeks out of the pouch, is already a fearless leaper.

443

Think Critically

1 Is "Rain Forest Babies" fiction or nonfiction? How can you tell? 🌀 FICTION AND NONFICTION

2 What are some ways in which all rain forests are alike? IMPORTANT DETAILS

3 Why does the author call rain forests "Earth's giant nursery"? AUTHOR'S CRAFT/IMAGERY

4 How are kangaroos and sugar gliders alike? How are they different? COMPARE AND CONTRAST

5 **WRITE** How do rain forest frogs protect themselves? Use details from the selection.

✏ SHORT RESPONSE

Meet the Author
Kathy Darling

Dear Reader,

I enjoy writing nonfiction books for children. I have written several books about science and about specific animals. I have traveled around the world to research animals for many of the books I have written.

Your friend,
Kathy Darling

GO online www.harcourtschool.com/storytown

Website

OUR WORLD
OF ANIMALS

WORLD OF
CONSERVATION

SUPPORT
THE ZOO

ZOO
MEMBERSHIP

EDUCATIONAL
PROGRAMS

OUR WORLD OF
ANIMALS

Baby Tapir Is Born!

A South American tapir has been born at the Houston Zoo. The Houston Zoo is in southeast Texas.

The 15-pound baby boy, Pico, was born to father, Nick, and mother, Casaba. Pico likes to wander off on his own.

Tapirs are the closest living relative of the rhinoceros. Tapirs live in the forests of South America. They are nocturnal, which means that they are active at night. They eat fruits, leaves, stems, branches, grasses, and tree bark.

HOUSTON
ZOO

NATURALLY
WILD

WOW!

A group of sea
lions in the water
is called a raft!

Live
Help

447

Connections

Comparing Texts

1 Could a tapir have been in "Rain Forest Babies"? Why or why not?

2 What rain forest baby do you want to learn more about? Why?

3 How do you think scientists learn about rain forest babies?

Phonics

Make Word Cards

On index cards, write words in which the letters *ir*, *ur*, *er*, or *ear* stand for the vowel sound in *turn*. Draw a picture on each card to show the word. Then share your word cards with a partner. Ask your partner to read each word.

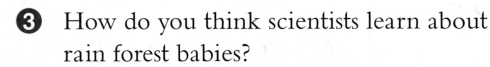

stir

Fluency Practice

Read with a Partner

Read "Rain Forest Babies" aloud with a partner. Take turns reading one page at a time. Be sure to read the headings, too. Without pausing, read groups of words that go together.

Writing

Write a Poem

With a partner, write sentences comparing each rain forest baby to something else using *as* or *like*. Use your sentences to write a poem about rain forest babies.

The macaw's feathers are <u>as</u> colorful <u>as</u> a rainbow.

The kangaroo kicks <u>like</u> a karate champ.

My Writing Checklist

Writing Trait → Conventions

✓ I use the words *as* and *like*.

✓ I use pronouns when I can.

Contents

Lesson 15
Theme Review and Vocabulary Builder

Readers' Theater
MYSTERY

A Birthday Mystery

Content-Area Reading
SCIENCE TEXTBOOK

YOUR Science TEXTBOOK

year

especially

enjoy

wear

interesting

question

wash

imagine

minute

father

Reading for Fluency

When you read a script aloud,

- group words together to read smoothly.

- use punctuation marks as clues to help you read smoothly and with feeling.

A Birthday Mystery

Characters

Narrator	Alex	Nicky
Pat	Sam	Lee

Setting

A house with birthday decorations

Narrator: Today is Alex's birthday.

Alex: My birthday is one of my favorite days of the year to celebrate. This year I'm especially excited because my family told me I'm going to get a special present.

Narrator: Alex can't wait to find out what the present is.

Alex: I know what I'll do! I'll ask my brothers and sisters for hints. I enjoy guessing games. If someone gives me hints, there's nothing I can't figure out.

453

Narrator: First, Alex asks Nicky.

Alex: Hi, Nicky. Why don't you give me a hint about my present?

Nicky: If I do, it won't be a surprise.

Alex: I'm not going to figure it out from one little hint.

Nicky: Okay, I'll give you one little hint. It's something that's very soft.

Alex: It's something that's soft? Maybe it's something that I can wear. Will you give me another hint?

Nicky: Alex, you said just one hint, and that's what you got. If you can't figure it out, you'll just have to wait.

Fluency Tip

Remember to pause briefly when you come to a comma.

Narrator: Next, Alex asks Pat.

Alex: Pat, why don't you give me a hint about what I'm getting for my birthday?

Pat: Gifts are supposed to be surprises. It wouldn't be much fun if I told you.

Alex: Please, just give me one little hint to make it interesting. I won't be able to figure out what it is from one hint.

Pat: Okay, I'll give you one little hint. It's something you can play with.

Alex: It's something I can play with? That could be anything. Can't you give me a better hint than that?

Pat: I gave you one hint, and that's all I'm going to tell you.

455

Narrator: Then Alex asks Sam.

Alex: Hey, Sam, why don't you give me a hint about my birthday present?

Sam: That would ruin the surprise. A present that isn't a surprise is not much fun.

Alex: It will still be a surprise. I'm not going to figure it out from one little hint.

Sam: Okay, here's one little hint. It's something that's hard to catch.

Alex: It's something that's hard to catch? Let me ask you one question. Is it a ball?

Sam: If I tell you, it won't be a surprise. Sorry, Alex. You're just going to have to wait.

Narrator: Last, Alex asks Lee.

Alex: Lee, how about giving me a hint about my present?

Lee: Presents should be surprises. You don't want to ruin your surprise, do you?

Alex: A hint won't ruin the surprise. I won't be able to figure out what the present is.

Lee: Okay, I'll give you one little hint. You sometimes have to wash it.

Alex: Now I'm really confused. I can't imagine what it could be if you have to wash it. Give me another hint, okay?

Lee: Sorry, Alex. You said one little hint. That's the only one you are going to get.

Fluency Tip

Let your voice rise at the end of questions that have a yes or no answer.

457

Narrator: Now it's time for the party.

Nicky: Alex, are you ready to find out what your present is? It's really special!

Alex: I sure am! I don't want to wait another minute.

Nicky: Remember, it's something very soft.

Pat: It's something you can play with.

Sam: It's hard to catch.

Lee: It also needs to be washed sometimes.

Alex: I give up. I know it's all of those things, but I can't guess what it is. May I have the present now?

Everyone: Okay, Alex, here it is!

Narrator: Alex's mother and father walk in with the present. His father puts it down, and it runs right over to Alex.

Fluency Tip

How would you group the words in these sentences? Read the lines that way.

Nicky: I told you that it was very soft!

Pat: I told you that it was something you could play with!

Sam: I told you that it was hard to catch!

Lee: I told you that you had to wash it sometimes!

Alex: You were all right. Those were all good clues, but there's just one hint you didn't give me.

Everyone: What's that?

Alex: That it would lick my face!

459

COMPREHENSION STRATEGIES
Review

Reading Your Science Book

Bridge to Content-Area Reading Science books have special features that help you read for information. Some of these features are labels, questions, and special vocabulary.

Read the notes on page 461. How can the features help you read a science lesson?

Review the Focus Strategies

The strategies you learned in this theme can help you read your science book.

Ask Questions

Ask yourself questions before, while, and after you read. What is this science lesson mostly about? What parts will give you answers to your questions?

Monitor Comprehension—Reread

Reread parts of a lesson you do not understand.

Use comprehension strategies as you read "The Life Cycle of a Frog" on pages 462–463.

VOCABULARY
New vocabulary words are in dark print. The meaning of the word is explained in the sentence. Vocabulary words are also in the glossary of your science book.

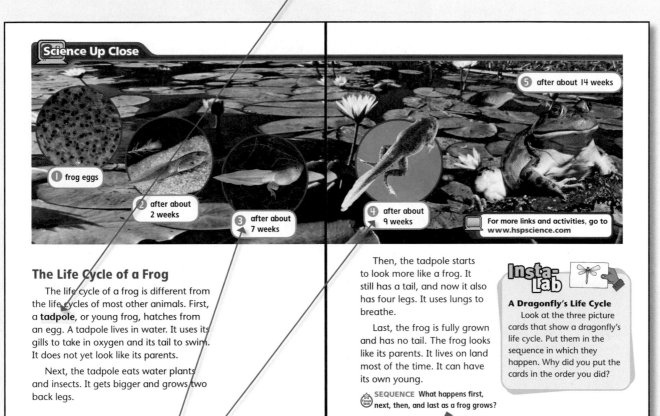

Science Up Close

1 frog eggs

2 after about 2 weeks

3 after about 7 weeks

4 after about 9 weeks

5 after about 14 weeks

For more links and activities, go to www.hspscience.com

The Life Cycle of a Frog

The life cycle of a frog is different from the life cycles of most other animals. First, a **tadpole**, or young frog, hatches from an egg. A tadpole lives in water. It uses its gills to take in oxygen and its tail to swim. It does not yet look like its parents.

Next, the tadpole eats water plants and insects. It gets bigger and grows two back legs.

Then, the tadpole starts to look more like a frog. It still has a tail, and now it also has four legs. It uses lungs to breathe.

Last, the frog is fully grown and has no tail. The frog looks like its parents. It lives on land most of the time. It can have its own young.

SEQUENCE What happens first, next, then, and last as a frog grows?

Insta-Lab

A Dragonfly's Life Cycle
Look at the three picture cards that show a dragonfly's life cycle. Put them in the sequence in which they happen. Why did you put the cards in the order you did?

60

61

LABELS
Labels tell what something is or describe parts of a diagram.

QUESTIONS
Questions at the ends of sections help you summarize.

Apply the Strategies Read these pages from a science book. As you read, stop and think about how you are using comprehension strategies.

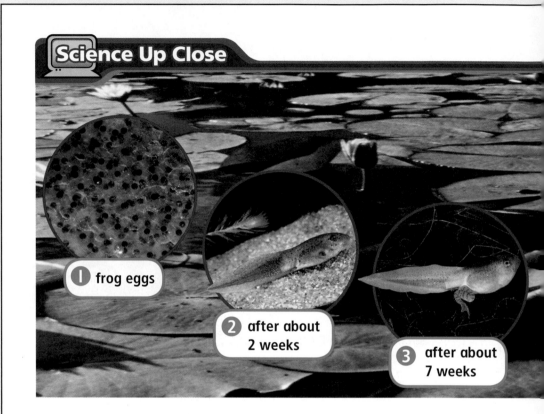

Science Up Close

1 frog eggs

2 after about 2 weeks

3 after about 7 weeks

The Life Cycle of a Frog

The life cycle of a frog is different from the life cycles of most other animals. First, a **tadpole**, or young frog, hatches from an egg. A tadpole lives in water. It uses its gills to take in oxygen and its tail to swim. It does not yet look like its parents.

Next, the tadpole eats water plants and insects. It gets bigger and grows two back legs.

60

462

Stop and Think

How did rereading help if you didn't understand part of the lesson? What questions do you still have?

5 after about 14 weeks

4 after about 9 weeks

For more links and activities, go to www.hspscience.com

Then, the tadpole starts to look more like a frog. It still has a tail, and now it also has four legs. It uses lungs to breathe.

Last, the frog is fully grown and has no tail. The frog looks like its parents. It lives on land most of the time. It can have its own young.

SEQUENCE What happens first, next, then, and last as a frog grows?

Insta-Lab

A Dragonfly's Life Cycle

Look at the three picture cards that show a dragonfly's life cycle. Put them in the sequence in which they happen. Why did you put the cards in the order you did?

61

Using the Glossary

Get to Know It!

The **Glossary** can help you read a word. You can look up the word and read it in a sentence. Some words have a picture to help you. The words in the **Glossary** are in ABC order.

Learn to Use It!

If you want to find *draw* in the **Glossary**, you should first find the **D** words. **D** is near the beginning of the alphabet, so the **D** words are near the beginning of the **Glossary**. Then you can use the guide words at the top of the page to help you find the entry word *draw*. It is on page 466.

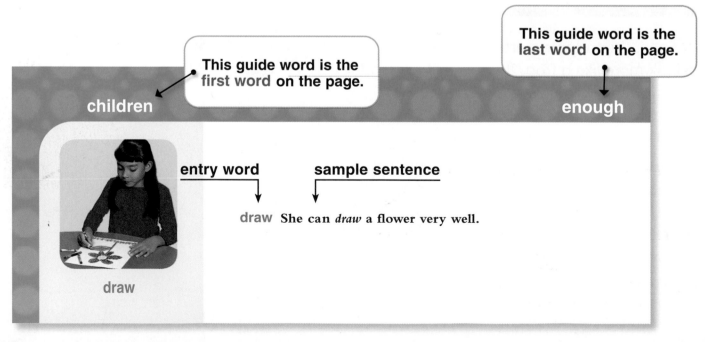

This guide word is the first word on the page.

This guide word is the last word on the page.

children

enough

entry word

sample sentence

draw She can *draw* a flower very well.

draw

A

a·bove The birds sit in a tree *above* the ground.

ac·cept Please *accept* this gift.

a·go Sherry left a long time *ago*.

al·read·y Have you *already* done your work?

B

be·lieve She does not *believe* that story.

bi·cy·cle Sonya's *bicycle* needs a new tire.

board The *board* had a nail in it.

bought Carmen's dad *bought* a new shirt for her.

broth·er John's *brother* is very tall.

brought He *brought* his lunch to school today.

C

care The art teacher does not *care* how long we take to finish.

caught He *caught* the fly ball!

cheer Keisha will *cheer* for the school's football team.

above

bicycle

cheer

cook

draw

ears

chil·dren The *children* were noisy.

clear The rain made it *clear* that we would not have a picnic today.

com·ing The storm is *coming* this way.

cook Dad will *cook* hot dogs on the grill.

cov·ered Be sure the picnic food is *covered*.

curve We could not see past the *curve* in the road.

dif·fer·ent His painting was *different* from the others.

draw She can *draw* a flower very well.

E

ear·ly The bus came *early* this morning.

ears The elephant's *ears* are huge.

eight Jamal is *eight* years old.

en·joy I *enjoy* any kind of pizza.

e·nough We have *enough* people for a kickball game.

es·pe·cial·ly The room was *especially* quiet.

eve·ry·thing Why is *everything* the same color?

ex·er·cise I like to *exercise* with my mom.

ex·pen·sive The computer was *expensive*.

F

---

fair It was a *fair* race, even though we lost.

fa·ther His *father* is a teacher at this school.

fa·vo·rite My *favorite* pet is a snake.

fi·nal·ly He *finally* stopped to tie his shoe.

G

---

guess *Guess* what I got for my birthday.

H

---

half Ron finished only *half* of his math work.

hun·dred This giant oak tree is about one *hundred* years old.

exercise

father

imagine

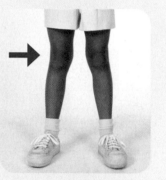

knee

laughed

I

i·de·a Anthony had an *idea* about how to fix the bike.

i·ma·gine *Imagine* how you will build your science project.

im·pos·si·ble The slide looked *impossible* to climb, but I did it!

in·ter·es·ting The movie about tigers was *interesting*.

K

knee When Sela fell down, she skinned her *knee*.

L

laughed I *laughed* when I saw the clown's floppy shoes.

learn It did not take very long to *learn* to play volleyball.

lose Dylan does not like to *lose* when he plays checkers.

M

mil·lion It looked as if a *million* stars were blinking in the sky.

min·ute In one *minute*, the bell will ring.

P

pic·ture When they took my *picture*, I forgot to smile.

po·lice The *police* officer was standing on the sidewalk.

po·pu·lar Basketball is a *popular* sport.

prove I had to *prove* to the coach that I was a good swimmer.

Q

ques·tion Sarah had a *question* about her math homework.

quite The class was *quite* ready for the party to begin.

S

shoes Lani tried on red *shoes* at the store.

short Ben's shoelace was too *short* to tie.

sign The *sign* pointed the wrong way.

some·times *Sometimes* when she falls, she cries.

picture

police

shoes

sugar

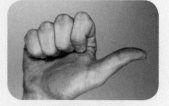

thumb

spe·cial You are a *special* friend.

straight Go *straight* down the hall and then turn left.

su·gar Eating a lot of *sugar* is not good for you.

sure I am *sure* that I have seen that before.

sweat The *sweat* was dripping down his face.

--- T ---

though The sun was shining, even *though* rain was still falling.

through A bee flew in *through* the open window.

thumb Tyrone got a paper cut on his *thumb*.

touch Do not *touch* anything on the teacher's desk.

tough Desert plants have a *tough* outer covering.

U

un·der·stand Do you *understand* how the tool works?

W

wash *Wash* that apple before you eat it.

wear Molly likes to *wear* dresses.

wo·man The *woman* in the purple dress is our principal.

woods The *woods* are filled with chirping birds.

world Today it is easy to travel around the *world*.

wor·ry Don't *worry* about the test.

Y

year My brother is one *year* older than I am.

young Juan is too *young* to cross the street alone.

wash

woman

woods

Index of Titles and Authors

Page numbers in green refer to biographical information.

Acknowledgments

For permission to reprint copyrighted material, grateful acknowledgment is made to the following sources:

Atheneum Books for Young Readers, an imprint of Simon & Schuster Children's Publishing Division: From *Henry and Mudge: The First Book* (Retitled: "Henry and Mudge") by Cynthia Rylant, illustrated by Suçie Stevenson. Text copyright © 1987 by Cynthia Rylant; illustrations copyright © 1987 by Suçie Stevenson.

BookStop Literary Agency and Gary Soto: Big Bushy Mustache by Gary Soto. Text copyright © 1998 by Gary Soto.

Candlewick Press, Inc., Cambridge, MA: Jamaica Louise James by Amy Hest, illustrated by Sheila White Samton. Text copyright © 1996 by Amy Hest; illustrations copyright © 1996 by Sheila White Samton.

Capstone Press: From *Friendliness* by Kristin Thoennes Keller. Text © 2005 by Capstone Press.

Joe Cepeda: Illustrations by Joe Cepeda from *Big Bushy Mustache* by Gary Soto. Illustrations copyright © 1998 by Joe Cepeda.

The Cricket Magazine Group, a division of Carus Publishing Company: "Reading with Your Fingers" from *CLICK* Magazine, November/December 2004. Text © 2004 by Carus Publishing Company.

Sam Curtis: "Rock-a-Bye Cows" by Sam Curtis from *Boys' Life* Magazine, September 1998. Published by the Boy Scouts of America.

Dial Books for Young Readers, A Division of Penguin Young Readers Group, A Member of Penguin Group (USA) Inc., 345 Hudson St., New York, NY 10014: The Great Ball Game: A Muskogee Story, retold by Joseph Bruchac, illustrated by Susan L. Roth. Text copyright © 1994 by Joseph Bruchac; illustrations copyright © 1994 by Susan L. Roth.

Farrar, Straus and Giroux, LLC: From *Gus and Grandpa and the Two-Wheeled Bike* by Claudia Mills, illustrated by Catherine Stock. Text copyright © 1999 by Claudia Mills; illustrations copyright © 1999 by Catherine Stock.

Harcourt, Inc.: "The Bat" from *beast feast* by Douglas Florian. Copyright © 1994 by Douglas Florian. "Changing" from *The Llama Who Had No Pajama* by Mary Ann Hoberman. Text copyright © 1981 by Mary Ann Hoberman.

HarperCollins Publishers: Winners Never Quit! by Mia Hamm, illustrated by Carol Thompson. Copyright © 2004 by Mia Hamm and Byron Preiss Visual Publications, Inc. "The Surprise" from *Frog and Toad All Year* by Arnold Lobel. Copyright © 1976 by Arnold Lobel.

Elizabeth Hauser: "Dogs" from *Around and About* by Marchette Chute. Text copyright 1957 by E. P. Dutton; text copyright renewed 1985 by Marchette Chute. Published by E. P. Dutton & Co.

Heinemann-Raintree, Chicago, IL: From *At Play: Long Ago and Today* by Lynette R. Brent. Text © 2003 by Heinemann Library, a division of Reed Elsevier Inc. *Dogs* by Jennifer Blizin Gillis. Text © 2004 by Heinemann Library, a division of Reed Elsevier Inc. From *Life As a Frog* by Victoria Parker. Text © 2004 by Raintree. Published by Raintree, a division of Reed Elsevier Inc.

Houghton Mifflin Company: "The Last Story: The Book" (Retitled: "The Book") from *George and Martha Back in Town* by James Marshall. Copyright © 1984 by James Marshall.

Houston Zoo: Logo and web site design from www.houstonzoo.org. Copyright © 2003-2006 by Houston Zoo, Inc.

Random House Children's Books, a division of Random House, Inc.: Arthur's Reading Race by Marc Brown. Copyright © 1996 by Marc Brown.

Marian Reiner: "A Lazy Thought" from *There Is No Rhyme for Silver* by Eve Merriam. Text copyright © 1962, 1990 by Eve Merriam.

Simon & Schuster Books for Young Readers, an Imprint of Simon & Schuster Children's Publishing Division: Click, Clack, Moo: Cows That Type by Doreen Cronin, illustrated by Betsy Lewin. Text copyright © 2000 by Doreen Cronin; illustrations © 2000 by Betsy Lewin.

TIME For Kids: "No Helmet? Pay Up!" from *TIME For Kids* Magazine, January 16, 1998.

Walker Publishing Company, Inc.: From *Rain Forest Babies* by Kathy Darling, photographs by Tara Darling. Text copyright © 1996 by Kathy Darling; photographs copyright © 1996 by Tara Darling.

Weekly Reader Corporation: From "Animals Have Special Jobs!" in *Weekly Reader* Magazine, Edition 2, Oct. 14, 2005. Text published and copyrighted by Weekly Reader Corporation.

Photo Credits

Placement Key: (t) top; (b) bottom; (l) left; (r) right; (c) center; (bg) background; (fg) foreground; (i) inset

14 The Hornby Train/1951-53,/Claude Maurice Rogers (1907-79) /Private Collection / The Bridgeman Art Library; 18 (t) C Squared Studios/Getty; 48 (bl) Bob West; 49 (bcl) Will & Deni McIntyre/Getty Images; 80 (bg) © Maximilian Weinzierl / Alamy; 81 (l) Wil Meinderts/Foto Natura/Minden; 82 (br) Kim Taylor & Jane Burton/Dorling Kindersley/Getty Images; 82 (br) Scott W. Smith/Animals Animals Earth Scenes; 83 (c)© ImageState / Alamy; 85 (cl) Design Pics Inc./Alamy; 85(r)Stephen Dalton/NHPA; 114 (br) Arthur Morris/ Corbis; 115 (tr) Jim Craigmyle/Corbis; 320 The Mukashi Collection /SuperStock; 327 (b) FoodCollection/Age Fotostock; 447 (r) Kevin Schafer/ Corbis.

All other photos © Harcourt School Publishers. Harcourt photos provided by Harcourt Index, Harcourt IPR, and Harcourt Photographers: Weronica Ankarorn, Eric Camden, Doug DuKane, Ken Kinsie, April Riehm and Steve Williams.

Illustration Credits

Cover Art; Laura and Eric Ovresat, Artlab, Inc.